THE POOR LAW IN IRELAND 1838-1948

VIRGINIA CROSSMAN

MIC LIBRARY
WITHDRAWN FROM STOCK

D1331259

Printed by
DUNDALGAN PRESS (W. Tempest) LTD.
2006

ISSN No. 0-947897-02-X
ISBN No. 978-0-947897-02-4

Coláiste
Mhuire Gan Smál
Luimneach

Class	941. 508)
Suff	CRO
MN	14001280

©
Published by
THE ECONOMIC AND SOCIAL HISTORY SOCIETY OF IRELAND

CONTENTS

For Maria

INTRODUCTION

If there is one thing that economic and social historians of modern Ireland agree upon, it is the existence of high levels of poverty and deprivation in both rural and urban areas throughout most of the nineteenth and twentieth centuries. A considerable number of Irish people experienced poverty and even more lived in fear of it. The extent of rural poverty decreased after the Famine, but large numbers of people continued to experience periodic distress. In cities such as Dublin, Cork and Limerick, low wages and high rents forced working class families to live in overcrowded, poor quality housing in conditions that became synonymous in middle-class minds with immorality and disease. How to respond to Irish poverty, and to the social problems associated with it, exercised the minds of politicians, economists and philanthropists throughout this period. Public concern at the extent of poverty in pre-Famine Ireland gave rise to extensive discussions over the desirability and feasibility of introducing a statutory system of poor relief. After more than three decades of inquiry and debate, the Irish poor law was passed by the Westminster parliament in 1838. This introduced a nationwide system of poor relief based on the workhouse and financed by a local property tax. The poor law remained the primary form of poor relief in Ireland until the 1920s, and in Northern Ireland until after the Second World War.

The popular view of the Irish poor law continues to be dominated by the image of the workhouse, 'the most hated and feared institution ever established in Ireland' (O'CONNOR). The poor law system was designed to be disciplinary and life within the workhouse was bleak and often oppressive. However, the tendency within Irish poor law history to focus principally on the period of the Famine, when workhouses were at their most overcrowded and chaotic, has obscured the extent to which the system changed over the period of its operation. By the end of the nineteenth century what had been established as a method of deterrence, intended to relieve destitution alone, had evolved into a broad-based welfare system encompassing poor relief, medical care, sanitation and social housing. Workhouses were now operating

1

primarily as a refuge for the elderly and infirm, and the sick. As a result their character and the regime within them changed. Moreover, as we shall see, the poor were by no means passive victims of the poor law. They were skilled at using the system to their own advantage, and they were prepared to take action if they felt their treatment was unacceptable or unjust.

Poor law history is an expanding field. Having initially concentrated mainly on institutional and administrative developments, poor law historians in Britain have broadened their focus to examine the experience of being poor and the complex strategies that poor people adopted in order to survive (KIDD; KING & TOMPKINS). An application for poor relief was generally resorted to only when all other means had failed. Historians have also explored regional variations in relief to determine whether the English poor law operated in different ways in different regions (KING). Irish poor law history is, by comparison, in its infancy. We know something about how the system developed and how it was administered, but little about its regional character or the experiences of those who used it. Nevertheless, there is now a considerable body of work on the poor law in Ireland ranging from histories of individual workhouses to studies of particular aspects of the relief system, such as the evolution of medical services. This pamphlet provides an overview of published research. The aim is to explain why the poor law was introduced, how it operated and how it changed over the course of the nineteenth and twentieth centuries. Details of the works cited can be found in the Bibliography under the name of the author, which appears in capitals in the text. Where a direct quotation is used, the page number is given in the text alongside the name of the author.

I

THE MAKING OF THE IRISH POOR LAW

(a) *Poverty and welfare in pre-Famine Ireland*
Poverty represented one of the most pressing social problems facing those responsible for the government of Ireland in the early nineteenth century. An almost continuous series of official and unofficial inquiries held in the first decades of the century presented a near uniform picture of widespread and acute deprivation. The human consequences of this situation, most evident in the crowds of beggars that filled country roads and towns, were regarded not alone as a cause of humanitarian concern but as a major political issue that affected the whole of the United Kingdom. For with growing numbers of Irish labourers migrating to Britain, Irish social problems were threatening to spill over into Britain at a time when the whole question of how far the state should intervene to relieve poverty was exercising the minds of the political classes.

It remains open to question whether the condition of the Irish peasantry - frequently claimed to be the worst in Europe - was as desperate as contemporaries assumed. MOKYR (p. 10) argues that Ireland was neither overpopulated nor poor in a traditional sense. It was rather a population that was 'comparatively well fed and well heated, but poorly housed and clad'. Analysis of the physical characteristics of soldiers and convicts suggests that the Irish enjoyed better nutritional standards and higher biological well-being than the English, although there were significant regional variations (Ó GRÁDA 1991; OXLEY). Trends in imported goods, and in literacy, suggest a rise in average living standards in the period between the Union and the Famine. Such developments, however, probably had little direct impact on the lives of the rural poor for whom, Ó GRÁDA (1994, p. 85) observes, 'immiseration is likely'.

Prior to 1838, Ireland had no statutory system of poor relief. This is not to say that there was no provision for the Irish poor.

During the eighteenth century the Irish parliament had passed enabling legislation allowing for the establishment and support of county infirmaries and houses of industry. By the end of the century major towns and cities throughout Ireland contained a variety of welfare institutions set up as a result of either private or municipal initiative. These included general and specialist hospitals, dispensaries, orphanages and asylums and a number of houses of industry or workhouses. The countryside was less well provided for but DICKSON (p. 157) has identified 'an old Irish poor law of sorts' operating at parish level through the Church of Ireland vestry, which constituted 'an active or potentially active welfare body', both in channelling alms to the endemically poor and in organising local charitable committees in really hard years'. However, since the Anglican community formed only a small proportion of the population outside the north and east, active vestries were largely confined to these areas. A similar regional imbalance is evident in the distribution of mendicity societies which also relied heavily on the contributions of well-to-do Protestants. Generally established in the early decades of the nineteenth century, and funded by voluntary contributions, mendicity societies provided various forms of assistance, from grants of food or money to the provision of shelter and, in some cases, employment (MacDOWELL 1956; MacATASNEY 2001). The largest mendicity institutions were those in Dublin and Belfast, both of which continued to operate after the introduction of the poor law, albeit on a smaller scale (WOODS; STRAIN). Unable to rely on either the voluntary sector or the state for assistance, the poor depended primarily on their own resources and those of their relatives and neighbours. Mutual aid was generally informal but self-help organizations did exist in the form of friendly societies, women's Dorcas societies, savings clubs and banks, and poor shops. By depositing small amounts of money in the Coolattin poor shop, for example, local residents were able to accumulate sums sufficient for the purchase of clothes, shoes and blankets (Ó CATHAOIR).

Those best provided for at this period were the sick poor. Indeed if there was an old Irish poor law it was to be found, one contemporary observer suggested in 1835, in the institutional relief provided by medical charities which conferred 'vast benefits' on the sick poor.[1] Historians have generally agreed, arguing that public health provision 'rivalled the best in Europe in the 1820 and 1830s' (Ó GRÁDA 1994, p. 97). Agencies catering for the well poor, on the other hand, were 'badly distributed, uncoordinated, and often ill-supported, and their united efforts were puny compared to the vast sum total of misery they were striving to alleviate' (McDOWELL 1956, p. 35). While the favourable assessment of institutions established for the relief of the sick poor has recently been challenged by GEARY, it remains the case that such institutions were far more common and more widely distributed than those available to the well poor, only a tiny minority of whom could hope to obtain any kind of relief. The focus on the sick poor reflected contemporary concerns about the spread of disease as well as a desire to direct assistance to those perceived to be most deserving of it. Prevailing ideas about poverty and welfare held that while the impotent poor – the very young, the very old and the sick and permanently disabled - were deserving of help, to assist anyone who was capable of supporting themselves was to encourage idleness and immorality.

The concept of the deserving and undeserving poor was central to welfare provision throughout this period. Whilst generally associated with middle class values and perceptions, and often assumed to be an English importation to Ireland, the concept became rooted in Irish popular culture. Ó CIOSÁIN has shown that ordinary people drew a distinction between fraudulent beggars, those who invented or exaggerated a disability for example, and those who were genuinely in need, seeing only the latter as deserving of charity. This distinction was reinforced by the Catholic church which, Ó CIOSÁIN (p. 99) maintains, 'was beginning to act as a powerful hegemonic institution, both inside and outside the state structures'. Catholic clergy frequently acted as the distributors and arbitrators of relief, placing themselves as the conduit of charity between the people and the poor.

As the limits of voluntarism were progressively exposed, the state became more involved in the relief of poverty and the prevention of disease. Public works schemes were introduced during periods of distress in 1816-17 and 1822-23 and a loan fund was established to advance money for public works that would provide employment for labourers. In 1831 responsibility for the distribution of government loans and grants for public works was entrusted to the newly constituted Board of Works. At the same time legislation was passed to enable grand juries to erect and support district fever hospitals, and a national board of health was established in 1820 to advise government on public health issues (McDOWELL 1956; GEARY). The poor law thus needs to be seen as one element in a pattern of state intervention in social and economic affairs. Such intervention generally involved the state taking on roles 'significantly different from those which it fulfilled in England' (Ó TUATHAIGH, p. 115), where the landed elite could generally be relied on to take responsibility for local administration. In Ireland, the failure of local magistrates to act effectively, either to maintain law and order or to provide efficient local government, had prompted successive administrations to introduce legislation establishing central boards to co-ordinate local action in matters such as health, education, and economic development, and assigning key elements of local responsibility to a cadre of centrally appointed professionals, such as assistant barristers and stipendiary magistrates (CROSSMAN 1996; O'BRIEN 1999). The poor law was unusual in that the administrative structures it created had originally been designed for and were already operational in England, but it followed the example of earlier Irish legislation in placing responsibility for the system as a whole in the hands of centrally appointed officials, the Poor Law Commissioners and their assistants.

Economic depression and popular disaffection in Britain in the post-Napoleonic war era had given fresh urgency to debates over the cost and efficacy of the system of poor relief that had been in operation since the beginning of the seventeenth century. Criticism of the existing system was heavily influenced by contemporary theories of political economy that held that any provision of poor relief to the able-bodied would tend to depress wage levels, stimulate population growth and damage familial and societal relationships. The 'new' English poor law of 1834 replaced the old system of parochial outdoor relief with a centrally directed, though locally administered, system based on the workhouse. English ideas on poverty in general, and on Irish poverty in particular, were to prove crucial in determining the nature and timing of the Irish poor law. Viewed from England, where the poor law was widely regarded as having helped to prevent revolution, an Irish poor law appeared to offer real advantages to a country apparently plagued with crime and disorder, and suffering from under-development and under-investment. The need to provide a safeguard against extremes of social deprivation thus overrode contemporary suspicion of tax-based welfare schemes as a drain on industry and an encouragement to laziness and improvidence (MITCHISON; INNES).

So long as the debate over the English poor law remained unresolved there was little incentive for ministers to take decisive action to address Irish poverty. Establishing a royal commission to investigate the condition of the poorer classes in Ireland chaired by the Protestant archbishop of Dublin, Richard Whately, allowed the Whig government to postpone the issue of Irish poverty until the shape of the English system had been determined (BURKE; CONWAY). Historians have been impressed by the diligence with which the Whately Commission set about its task, collecting statistics on everything from wage rates to existing methods of relief, and interviewing over 1,500 people (MOKYR). The eventual report ran to around half a million words (McDOWELL 1956). Having found almost 2.5 million people, or 30 per cent of the Irish population, to be in distress for part of the year, the commissioners concluded that any system of organised relief, except for the impotent poor, would be impractical and excessively expensive. Instead, they recommended an extensive programme of economic development ranging from assisted emigration to the establishment of model agricultural schools. Whilst praising the ambitious nature of these proposals, most historians have acknowledged that they were too complex, too costly and too long-term to appeal to ministers, particularly ministers with a small parliamentary majority (MACINTYRE; McDOWELL 1956; BURKE; MacDONAGH). Indeed with hindsight, one could conclude that the weight of documentation bore an inverse proportion to the likelihood of the report's recommendations being implemented.

What ministers wanted was a measure that could be implemented quickly and cheaply. It is hardly surprising, therefore, that they opted to extend the reformed English poor law to Ireland, as advocated by the English poor law commissioner George Nicholls, rather than embrace the programme of measures recommended by the Whatley Commission. After a swift tour of Ireland in the autumn of 1836 to assess the practicability of his plan, Nicholls concluded that the workhouse system could be safely applied to Ireland. He proposed the erection of around 80 workhouses across the country, supported by a local rate and administered by boards of guardians operating under the supervision and control of a central authority. Relief would be available only in the workhouse, thus making the system simpler to administer and acting as a test of destitution, since only someone driven by actual necessity would voluntarily submit themselves to the restrictions that applied there (NICHOLLS). Historians have judged both Nicholls and the Irish poor law harshly. Nicholls is accused of spending too little time in Ireland and of taking too rosy a view of its economy (BURKE; KINEALY 1994). Yet, as he himself noted, there would have been little point in duplicating the Whately Commission's research. His brief was to assess the viability of the workhouse system and in fulfilling this he produced proposals that were, in stark contrast to those of the Whately Commission, 'lucid, assured and highly practical' (McDOWELL 1989, p. 556). And while BURKE ridicules his claim that the condition of Ireland had been improving over the previous thirty years, modern economic historians have broadly endorsed this view (MOKYR & Ó GRÁDA; GUINNANE). Nicholls' positive assessment in fact echoed that of the Whatley Commission, which expressed considerable optimism about Irish agricultural improvement.

As a welfare provision, the poor law has been condemned as unsuitable and ineffective. MACINTYRE (p. 226) criticised the measure as a piece of 'doctrinaire legislation' by which a welfare system appropriate for an economy 'offering a wide range of alternative employment outside agriculture' was applied to a country whose economy was characterised by 'chronic under-employment and periodic mass destitution'. The act was an 'impracticable and even harmful luxury'. MacDONAGH (pp. 227-8) took this argument one step further by claiming that the English poor law was 'inappropriate even for England and Wales' and was even more so for Ireland, where 'virtually no demand was matched by a practically limitless supply'. As a consequence the Irish poor law 'failed to deal seriously with the effects, not to add the causes, of poverty or to provide a relief system nearly adequate for the famine that struck within two years of its completion', and was to develop into a 'massive instrument of depopulation', an allegation previously made by the economic historian G. O'BRIEN (1921). But the poor law was never intended to deal with the causes of poverty, and certainly not with famine conditions. NICHOLLS (p. 177) expressly stated that famine conditions were 'beyond the powers of a poor law to provide for'. It is true that the poor law did promote depopulation during the Famine, but this was the result of the Gregory clause passed in 1847 which was not part of the original act. Thus whilst its framers can be criticised for viewing the relief of poverty in too narrow and doctrinaire a way, it is important to recognise what the poor law was and was not intended to achieve. Far from believing the workhouse system to be 'the saviour of the whole economy' (KINEALY 1994, p. 22), Nicholls never expected the act to work an economic miracle in Ireland (BURKE; McDOWELL 1989). He envisaged it as helping the country through the transition from a subsistence to a wage economy. Moreover, neither Nicholls nor the government conceived the poor law operating in isolation. Nicholls also advocated assisted emigration as a way of reducing Ireland's surplus population; ministers had originally hoped to accompany the poor relief bill with a measure providing for large-scale, state-financed railway construction.

GRAY (p. 32) has argued that the adoption of the Irish poor law represented more than 'a simple desire for institutional anglicization', being a key element of the 'justice for Ireland' policy of the progressive 'Foxite whigs' led by Lord John Russell. The poor law had the support of many O'Connellite MPs, as well as most Catholic clergy, and was strongly opposed by Irish landowners. It can therefore plausibly be seen as a positive attempt to address a recognised social evil. However, a poor law had never formed part of the programme of reform measures that O'Connell demanded of the Whigs. And while Russell and his colleagues may have been genuine in their desire to 'do good in Ireland', and were clearly concerned about Irish poverty, they were not concerned enough to commit to paying for its relief. One of the great attractions of the English model for ministers was the fact that much of the cost would fall on Irish landlords, who were widely believed to have neglected their duty to provide for the less fortunate in Irish society (KINEALY 1994; GRAY).

(b) *The Irish Poor Law Act 1838*
NICHOLLS (p. 176) was anxious that the Irish poor law should 'assimilate in all respects as nearly as possible to that established in England', although he recognised that some variations would be necessary to accommodate the 'different circumstances' of the two countries. The effect of these variations was to establish a harsher relief system than operated in England, and one that adhered more closely to the principles underlying the new English poor law (KINEALY 1994). English poor law reformers had hoped to eliminate outdoor relief for the able-bodied and their families, but had failed to get this provision through parliament. Consequently, the workhouse test was provisional rather than mandatory in England. In Ireland, all applicants whatever their circumstances were required to enter the workhouse. Furthermore, guardians were under no obligation to provide additional relief once the workhouse was full. In one important respect, however, the Irish law was less restrictive than the English. In the absence of a law of settlement, applicants could claim relief from any board of guardians, and so long as they were destitute and there was room in the workhouse, guardians were obliged to admit them. English and Scottish guardians, by contrast, were obliged to relieve only the local poor. Applicants who could not establish 'residency' in a union were liable to be forcibly removed to their place of birth, or in the case of Irish immigrants to the most convenient Irish seaport (KINEALY 1994).

As in England, the poor law in Ireland was administered by boards of guardians, composed of the elected representatives of the ratepayers, and local magistrates. The latter, known as ex officio guardians, initially comprised one third, later increased to one half, of the total board (CROSSMAN 1994). Overall responsibility for the Irish poor law system was entrusted to the English Poor Law Commissioners, administrative uniformity and efficiency being judged more important than national feeling. The practical operation of the system was overseen by a resident commissioner in Dublin, assisted by eight assistant commissioners. Since it was believed that little confidence could be placed in either the diligence or the competence of Irish local administrators, the Poor Law Commissioners were given greater regulatory powers in Ireland than they possessed in England. In the event of an Irish board of guardians failing to discharge its duties effectually, the Commissioners could dissolve the board and place the administration of the union in the hands of paid officers.

Even the harshest critics of Nicholls' approach to poor relief have praised the energy and efficiency with which he set about implementing the Irish relief act (BURKE; KINEALY 1994). By the time he left Ireland in 1842, the country had been divided into 130 unions and workhouses had either been built or were under construction in all of them. The task of designing and supervising the construction of the workhouses was entrusted to the young English architect George Wilkinson. Wilkinson produced a simple plan that could be adapted to accommodate anything from 200 to 2,000 inmates. Most Irish workhouses were in the medium range category with accommodation for between 500 and 900 people. The total capacity of the 130 workhouses constructed or adapted under Wilkinson's direction was around 94,000. Despite being built to a standard design, the preferences of local guardians and the use of local materials and workmen meant that individual workhouses often displayed distinctive features. The Carlow workhouse, for example, which incorporated a number of Italianate features, was designed to blend in with other public buildings in the town. Perhaps inevitably, given the scale of the building programme and the speed with which it was undertaken, costs rose and there were complaints about the standards of workmanship. The buildings were generally structurally sound, indeed many of them are still standing, but there were numerous problems with fixtures and furnishings, ranging from poorly fitted windows and gates to inadequate drainage and ventilation (McDOWELL 1956).

As the appointment of first Nicholls and then Wilkinson indicates, ministers and officials made few concessions to local sentiment. The hectoring tone adopted by the Poor Law Commissioners in their communications, and their fondness for lecturing local guardians about their duties, caused considerable resentment (O'BRIEN 1986). This insensitivity reflected a sense of moral purpose. The Commissioners, McDOWELL (1956, p. 52) suggests, saw themselves as not merely 'departmental officials engaged in guaranteeing the indigent Irish man from starvation, but warriors in a great administrative crusade'. Yet despite possessing a powerful armoury in the shape of the poor law regulations, the Commissioners found themselves at a disadvantage in their battle to achieve national uniformity. Since responsibility for the practical operation of poor law legislation lay with local boards, the poor law came to be 'continuously modified as the result of the character of individual unions and their local administrators' (KINEALY 1992, p. 580).

Accounts of the early years of the poor law have highlighted the extent of opposition both to the principle of the act and to interference by the Poor Law Commissioners in the conduct of local affairs (O'BRIEN 1986; KINEALY & MacATASNEY). The Irish medical profession successfully resisted attempts to place local dispensaries and fever hospitals under the control of the Poor Law Commissioners by mobilising anti-poor law sentiment amongst both medical practitioners and Irish landowners (CASSELL; GEARY). From an English perspective, however, any problems encountered in Ireland were no more than minor local difficulties. In contrast to the sustained resistance offered to the Poor Law Commissioners in Wales and the north of England, where guardians refused to build workhouses or appoint officials, so that as late as 1854 18 unions had failed to build workhouses, verbal opposition was rarely converted into action in Ireland, allowing the fabric and machinery of the poor law to be established largely without incident. There was a brief period in the early 1840s when it looked as though hostility to poor rates might provoke a wave of popular agitation in the Irish countryside comparable to the resistance to tithe payments in the 1830s (O'BRIEN 1988; MacDONAGH). During 1842-3 a number of unions experienced serious difficulties in collecting poor rates. The assistance of the police or the military was required in 21 unions in the period from January 1843 to January 1844 to protect rate collectors and enforce rate collections (CROSSMAN 1994). Hoping to exploit anti-poor law sentiment, O'Connell included abolition of the poor law in his Repeal manifesto and made public appeals to the Irish gentry to join a campaign to get the new law either modified or repealed. However, poor rates were always going to form a shaky foundation for a great popular campaign since so many within the Irish party and the country supported the idea if not the form of the poor law (MACINTYRE; McCAFFREY). When small landholders were relieved of the immediate burden of rates in 1843, what little revolutionary potential the issue had contained drained away.

It is difficult to know what the poor felt about the system since their views were not recorded. MACINTYRE (pp. 233-4) concluded that the poor 'or that small proportion of them who came into contact with the system, seem to have accepted the workhouses'. O'BRIEN (1986), on the other hand, believes that the poor rejected workhouses as incompatible with Irish popular culture, cultural acceptance of begging leading the poor to regard themselves as entitled to outdoor relief. However, dislike of the workhouse is not the same as rejection of it. People may have entered the workhouse as a last resort, but they did enter. Once inside dissatisfaction with the conditions imposed, and in particular with the diet provided, sometimes led people to riot. The substitution of potatoes for bread at breakfast prompted serious disorder amongst the women inmates of Cork workhouse in 1840, for example (O'BRIEN 1985). But this suggests a refusal to accept the way the workhouse was run rather than its existence. Here again comparison with England is instructive. Hostility to the new English poor law prompted periodic outbreaks of popular agitation in the form of large-scale riots, arson attacks on workhouses and threats against local officials (DIGBY; BRUNDAGE). Such incidents are almost unknown in Ireland, an absence that seems all the more significant given the country's long history of popular disturbances. There appear to have been no arson attacks on Irish workhouses in the pre-Famine period, for example, despite a tradition of rural incendiarism. Moreover, anti-poor law agitation in England and Wales tended to focus on the operation of the relief system, protests being sparked by, for example, the withdrawal of outdoor relief or the introduction of workhouse classification. Popular resistance in Ireland focused on the financial burden imposed by the new law, and it was rate collectors, not poor law guardians or workhouse officials, who attracted popular ire. This point should not be pressed too far, since poor rates were clearly representative of the system they supported, but it is difficult not to suspect that Irish tenants were more concerned about their own pockets than about the treatment of the poor.

(c) *The relief system prior to the Famine*
Life within an Irish workhouse was highly regulated, the intention being to promote obedience, industry and self-control within the inmates. On admittance paupers were cleansed, clothed in workhouse uniform and classified. Men were separated from women, children from adults, and the sick from the able-bodied. Some workhouses also had separate accommodation for single mothers and prostitutes. The Irish workhouse diet was designed to be monotonous and frugal. The Poor Law Commissioners laid down minimum food allowances for a diet of two meals a day to consist of a combination of potatoes, oatmeal, brown bread, milk and soup. Children were allowed three meals daily, as were paupers in Ulster, three meals being perceived as customary amongst Ulster labourers (O'BRIEN 1986; CRAWFORD 1993). Unless sick or disabled, all paupers were required to work. For some this meant contributing to the upkeep of the workhouse through domestic work or gardening. For others it meant hours devoted to tedious, repetitive tasks such as breaking stones or picking oakum. Children were expected to attend school either within the workhouse or in the local national school for a few hours each day, the rest of their time being devoted to physical work around the workhouse. Paupers were expected to be quiet and orderly. Disrespectful or disorderly behaviour was liable to

punishment either by extra work or by reduction of rations. Those who committed repeated or more serious misdemeanours, such as stealing or damaging work house property, or assaulting either another inmate or a member of the staff, were liable to be confined in the punishment cell for up to 24 hours, or sent before the local magistrates. A well regulated workhouse depended on competent, responsible staff. Where these were lacking regulations were not always adhered to and discipline could be lax.

The poor law was intended to operate free from political or sectarian feeling. To this end clergymen were excluded from membership of poor law boards and workhouse chaplains were required to restrict their activities to inmates of their own religious persuasion. Such precautions failed to prevent the frequent accusations of proselytism that embittered both inter-denominational relations within the workhouses and the relation-ship between the Catholic church and the poor law authorities. The church also resented the fact that while most inmates were Catholic, the vast majority of workhouse staff were Protestant. Further controversy was caused by the legal ruling made in 1842 that foundlings whose religion was unknown should be brought up as Protestants (ROBINS; BURKE).

Despite the efforts expended in seeking to discipline and subdue Irish paupers, many refused to accommodate themselves to a life of regulation and restraint. They were disrespectful to workhouse staff. They left the workhouse without permission and returned drunk. They altered workhouse clothes to make them more comfortable and less standardized. They rioted if the food was inedible. They received visitors on the wards who brought in food and other items. They complained to the authorities about poor conditions and ill-treatment. They also became adept at utilising the relief system. Vagrants entered the workhouse on Saturday evening and left the following Monday thus avoiding having to work. Women declared themselves deserted in order to enter the workhouse with their children while their husbands sought work as migrant labourers, or applied for admittance to a particular workhouse in order to take advantage of an assisted emigration scheme. It is important, therefore, not to see paupers purely as victims of an oppressive system (McLOUGHLIN 2002). Entering the workhouse was just one of the strategies that poor people adopted in order to survive and should not be assumed to define either the individuals or their experiences.

Analyses of the relief system in the pre-Famine period are limited in number and scope, but the general picture is plain. Few workhouses held anything near their full capacity. The Cavan workhouse, which had a capacity of 1,200, contained 541 inmates at the beginning of 1844, while Midleton in County Cork (capacity 800) contained 339 (Ó GRÁDA 1994). The exceptions were large urban workhouses such as the South Dublin Union workhouse (capacity 2,000), that became full within months of opening (BURKE). Examination of the indoor registers of a number of unions across the country reveals that workhouses contained more women than men and roughly equal numbers of sick and able-bodied. Children together with the elderly made up the majority of workhouse inmates (BURKE; Ó GRÁDA 1994; Ó CATHAOIR). Adult paupers were generally unskilled, the most commonly recorded occupations being labourer for men and servant for women (O'BRIEN 1986). Most inmates were either single or had lost their spouse through death or desertion, indicating that marriage provided some degree of economic security. Compared to those receiving relief in England at the same period, the totality of Irish paupers included a slightly lower proportion of women and a slightly higher proportion of sick and disabled. This reflects the restrictive nature of Irish poor relief and reinforces Ó GRÁDA's conclusion (1994, p. 98) that the system was 'functioning broadly as intended by those who devised it'. Only the most vulnerable members of society - those unable to support themselves - either sought or received admission to Irish workhouses.

But if the workhouse system was successful in discouraging the poor from seeking relief, its effectiveness in other respects has been called into question. The ultimate test of the 'adequacy and suitability' of the poor law, O'BRIEN (1986, pp. 132-4) has argued, lay in the 'close application of its rules within the walls of union workhouses' and in this respect it 'must be deemed to have failed in its intended purposes'. Conceding that the framework of the poor law was successfully established, he argues that 'the accompanying spirit of austerity, efficiency, inflexible discipline and strict economy all buckled and broke against the reluctance and resentment of Irish guardians and Irish ratepayers'. BURKE similarly portrays the tension between the orderly plans of the central poor law authorities and the chaotic state of local unions as proof that the poor law was fundamentally unsuited to Ireland.

Evidence of maladministration and inefficiency is not hard to find. All too often Irish guardians were more concerned to keep poor rates low than to provide adequate care for the paupers in their charge. Buildings were poorly equipped and maintained and dietaries inadequate. Furthermore, the tendency to employ people as union officials on the basis of connections rather than qualifications resulted in some very unsuitable people being appointed. Between 1843 and 1852, the Poor Law Commissioners were obliged to dismiss around 70 workhouse masters, 25 matrons, 60 schoolmasters and 20 schoolmistresses (ROBINS). However, since many of the examples of maladministration cited by historians are drawn from official reports, it could equally well be argued that, far from failing, the system was operating effectively and that, where problems existed, these were identified and addressed. The number of officers dismissed undoubtedly indicates poor recruitment procedures, but it also suggests that incompetent or abusive behaviour was not tolerated. The supervisory role of the central authorities was intended to promote good practice amongst local authorities throughout the United Kingdom. It was never envisaged that this process would happen overnight. For, if English local authorities required guidance, how much more in need of instruction were those in Ireland, where society was assumed to be less developed?

Given their experience of English local authorities, it seems unlikely that the Poor Law Commissioners were unprepared for the problems they encountered in Ireland. Boards of guardians both in the north of England and in Wales never fully accepted the idea of the workhouse test and successfully resisted any strict application of it (BRUNDAGE; KING). In the early years of the system, Irish poor law guardians were rarely so intractable. Having less practical experience of administering poor relief, they had

had less opportunity to acquire bad habits, such as relying too much on outdoor relief, and were more open to central direction. They were also more constrained by statutory regulations. English guardians could refuse to implement the workhouse test and could continue to offer the majority of claimants outdoor relief, and there was nothing the Poor Law Commissioners could do about it. Irish boards of guardians had only one form of relief available to them, the workhouse, and boards that flouted poor law regulations could be dissolved.

Workhouse organisation tended to adhere more closely to the new poor law template in Ireland than in England, if only because the adoption of a standard design made it easier to enforce the regulations on classification which required the separation of different classes of pauper. Many English workhouses had been built under the old poor law with no provision for separate accommodation, and often proved difficult to adapt. Throughout the United Kingdom the workhouse system was characterised by diversity and there were examples of good and bad management in every region. In Ireland, some guardians operated what was seen as too lenient a regime, others what was seen as too harsh. Thus the Poor Law Commissioners found themselves urging the guardians of Rathdrum Union to increase the quality and quantity of food provided in the workhouse, whilst rebuking those of Lismore and Waterford for excessively generous allowances (KINEALY 1992; Ó CATHAOIR). Conditions in many Irish workhouses were deplorable, but there was nothing in this period to compare with the Andover scandal in Hampshire when famished paupers were reduced to gnawing on the bones they were meant to be grinding into meal.

II

THE POOR LAW DURING THE GREAT FAMINE

(a) *The administration of poor relief*
The period of the Great Famine (1845-52) is the one period for which we have abundant evidence about the operation of the Irish poor law. Local historians have explored the workings of a considerable number of individual unions, whilst academics have analysed the efficacy of relief administration both locally and nationally. The picture that has emerged from this extensive body of work is one of striking contrasts and significant variations. All parts of the country suffered from the effects of the Famine but districts in the south and west were particularly badly hit. These were areas where rateable values were low, where small-holdings predominated, and where the majority of the population were dependent on the potato as their main source of food. At the same time, however, some unions in the poorest areas managed to weather the storm better than might have been expected, while some of those in relatively prosperous areas experienced higher than average mortality rates. Exactly why this is remains unclear, but crucial factors appear to have been prevailing social and economic conditions, patterns of migration, the quality of local administration and leadership, and elements of chance. The chronology of the crisis also varied in different parts of the country, with the worst effects being over in the north and east by 1848 while the condition of parts of the south and west continued to deteriorate until 1850.

When the potato blight first became apparent the Poor Law Commissioners resisted calls for the poor law to be extended. They believed that it was vital to maintain a distinction between the relief of exceptional distress and ordinary poor relief, in order to prevent the poor law from being diluted by temporary measures, and to maintain the primacy of the workhouse test. Thus the official response to the appearance of the potato blight in 1845 was to follow the course that had been successfully

19

adopted in response to localised distress in 1839 and 1842 (KINEALY 1994). Public works were established to provide employment and some additional food supplies were imported into the country. In addition, relief committees under the guidance of a central Temporary Relief Commission were established in November 1845, and poor law guardians were instructed to make provision for outbreaks of fever in their localities by acquiring or erecting a suitable building, separate from the workhouse, that could be used as a fever hospital. The following year a temporary fever act created local boards of health together with a central supervisory body comprising five commissioners and two medical officers. The commissioners were reappointed in 1847 and a second temporary act passed to provide for the erection of fever hospitals in unions where these were lacking. By September 1847 there were 26,378 people in fever hospitals (O'NEILL 1956).

Poor law boards found that pressure on workhouse accommodation increased only gradually, with the numbers within workhouses rising from a little over 38,000 in December 1845 to around 51,000 in June 1846 (KINEALY 1994). Since workhouses could accommodate a total of over 90,000 paupers, this left considerable spare capacity. Some unions saw very little increase until later on. The most obvious impact of the Famine was less on numbers than on the workhouse diet, as most boards began to replace potatoes with other sources of food such as bread, oatmeal, rice and, increasingly, Indian meal. Many unions resorted to feeding paupers primarily on soup or stirabout made from a mixture of oatmeal and Indian meal. As financial pressures increased due to the difficulty of getting rates in, the diet tended to deteriorate and inmates often received inadequate nourishment. Diseases caused by vitamin deficiency such as scurvy and opthalmia became more common, particularly amongst paupers who had been resident in the workhouse for six months or more. Some inmates were driven to seek alternative accommodation. The prison authorities believed that mounting levels of insubordination within some workhouses were due to inmates committing misdemeanours with the express aim of being transferred to gaol, where conditions were better (CRAWFORD 1993).

Local studies have revealed both the common problems facing poor law boards and the disparate nature of guardians' responses to the crisis. Admissions to workhouses increased rapidly in December 1846 and January 1847. By February 1847 workhouses in 93 unions contained more people than they had been built to accommodate and some held more than double their intended capacity (O'NEILL 1956). Conditions within many workhouses became even more uncomfortable and unpleasant than usual, as well as providing ideal breeding grounds for contagious diseases. Supplies of bedding and clothing were often inadequate and medical officers despaired of the tendency to re-use the clothes of deceased paupers without ensuring that they had been properly cleaned and dried. Pressure of numbers meant that many of the regulations governing life within the workhouse could no longer be enforced and inmates of different sexes and ages found themselves sharing the same crowded spaces (O'NEILL 1956). The use of auxiliary buildings caused further disruption as paupers were moved between buildings. In Cashel Union, for example, 700 boys walked the four miles from an auxiliary workhouse in Castlelake to the main house in Cashel every Sunday to attend mass (LANIGAN).

With so many people requiring assistance, many boards of guardians began providing food relief outside the workhouse, even though this was contrary to poor law regulations. During the winter of 1846-47 almost half of the country's poor law boards were administering some form of outdoor relief (KINEALY 1994). The Poor Law Commissioners were strongly opposed to the granting of any outdoor relief and reminded guardians that to do so was 'quite contrary to the intention and spirit of the Poor Relief Act' and was liable to 'great abuse and confusion' (LANIGAN, p. 59). Guardians were well aware that their actions were illegal but argued, in the words of Callan guardians, that 'the circumstances of the utter destitution of the people' necessitated the provision of food.[2] In order to try to dissuade boards from resorting to outdoor relief, from December 1846 the Commissioners authorised guardians to provide extra accommodation if the workhouse became full, whilst warning them that they would have to meet the cost from the rates (DONNELLY).

Guardians accomplished this in a variety of ways, most commonly by erecting temporary sheds in the grounds of the workhouse or by hiring empty buildings in the locality. Many auxiliary buildings were ill suited to the purpose providing cramped, poorly ventilated accommodation. In some unions, however, the establishment of an auxiliary workhouse enabled guardians to remove their most vulnerable inmates to a healthier environment. The guardians of Tipperary Union transferred schoolchildren to an auxiliary workhouse at Greenane away from the main town, where they were spared the worst effects of the Famine (LANIGAN).

Women and children predominated amongst workhouse inmates during the Famine. By 1851, around 70 per cent of the total workhouse population in Cork was female while children made up 43 per cent of inmates over the first six months of 1847, compared to 36 per cent in 1845 (O'MAHONY). Children accounted for 63 per cent of workhouse inmates in Armagh in November 1848 along with 27 per cent adult women and 10 per cent adult men (GRANT). In South Dublin however, children appear to have formed a considerably smaller proportion of the total. BURKE cites a figure of 30 per cent for 1848. This discrepancy may partly be due to statistical factors since BURKE's figures are derived from a random sample of admissions while others refer to total admissions, but probably also reflects the number of adults moving into the capital. Mortality rates among children were very high. Child fatalities accounted for 44 per cent of total workhouse fatalities in 1845-6, and 53 per cent in 1847 (O'MAHONY).

The number of deaths within Irish workhouses rose from less than 6,000 in 1845 to over 14,000 in 1846 and 66,000 in 1847. Mortality rates were highest in the extreme west and lowest in Dublin and the north east (Ó GRÁDA 1994). The number of workhouse deaths peaked in April 1847 when 2.5 per cent of the inmates of Irish workhouses died in the space of a week (O'NEILL 1956). Thereafter mortality rates declined, though an outbreak of cholera in the spring of 1849 saw workhouse fatalities in unions outside Ulster reach their highest level since 1847. DONNELLY (p. 320) attributes the decline in mortality to the establishment of separate fever hospitals, the increase in the number of dispensaries, the expansion of workhouse accommodation, and the granting of outdoor relief. The provision of additional accommodation was, he maintains, prompted by reasons of 'economy not of humanity' since it enabled guardians to apply the workhouse test and thus limit the amount of outdoor relief provided.

During 1846-47 government policy on famine relief underwent fundamental revision. Having replaced Peel's Conservative administration in the summer of 1846, the Whig government became increasingly dissatisfied with existing relief schemes. Despite the expenditure of around £5 million, relief was not reaching all those who needed it and there were growing reports of widespread abuses. Ministers were anxious to reduce the level of abuse, limit expenditure and provide more effectual relief. They were also anxious to ensure that the British taxpayer did not have to contribute more than a modest proportion of the bill. It was therefore decided to abandon the policy of keeping famine relief separate from ordinary relief, a distinction which had in any event become increasingly blurred, and to make the poor law responsible for both. This would ensure that relief was provided and paid for locally, thus encouraging landlords to take a more active role in its organisation. As an interim measure, during the period of changeover from public works to poor relief, the government established a nationwide network of soup kitchens to supply cooked food to the destitute. The administrative machinery established under the temporary relief, or soup kitchens, act of 1847 utilised the geographical divisions of the poor law as well as its personnel. Responsibility for distributing food lay with local relief committees made up of poor law guardians, magistrates, clergymen, ratepayers and the relief inspector for the district. By demonstrating 'what the Victorian state was capable of when it mobilized its human and financial resources' (GRAY, p. 266), the soup kitchen regime provides telling evidence that 'the relief framework could have been marshalled to distribute more aid' (Ó GRÁDA 1994, p. 197). What was lacking was not the bureaucratic framework or administrative expertise but the political will.

The Irish poor law had been designed as a residual or minimalist system. In order to make provision for more general relief, the original 1838 act had to be extended. The poor law extension act of 1847 enabled boards of guardians to give outdoor relief to anyone unable to work due to age, disability or ill-health, together with orphans and widows with two or more legitimate children. The able-bodied poor were still to be relieved within the workhouse unless circumstances made this impossible; if, for example, the workhouse was full or a site of infection. At the same time a duty was placed on poor law guardians to make provision for the relief of all destitute poor persons in their locality. O'NEILL (1956) interpreted the act as recognising the right of the destitute to support. KINEALY (1994) points out, however, that a right to relief was conferred only on those groups within the poor who qualified for outdoor relief, a much more limited entitlement. Passed at the same time, the poor law administration act established a separate poor law authority for Ireland comprising a resident chief commissioner acting together with the Chief Secretary and under secretary. Supervision of poor law boards was entrusted to salaried inspectors in place of the assistant commissioners who had formerly performed this function. By giving the Chief Secretary and under secretary a direct input into poor law administration, the new arrangements were intended to ensure effective co-ordination between the various branches of the Irish government; they also made it likely that the Irish Poor Law Commission would be drawn more closely into the politics of Irish administration than its predecessor.

The 1847 extension act, like the original 1838 act, was a compromise measure. It supporters included O'Connellite MPs and the Irish Catholic clergy who saw an extended poor law as essential if adequate aid was to be provided. Its opponents included Irish landowners worried about the drain on their revenues, and die-hard opponents of outdoor relief such as Whately, Nassau Senior and Monteagle, who argued that relief outside the workhouse could never be administered safely in Ireland since the demand for it would be too great, resulting in spiralling costs, the demoralisation of the poor and the impoverishment of ratepayers. Perhaps the most significant amendment to the bill during its passage through parliament was the addition of a clause, later known as the Gregory clause, prohibiting holders of more than a quarter of an acre of land from receiving relief. The intention was to prevent abuse, to encourage the consolidation of land and to promote the conversion of small-holders into wage labourers. Accepted with reluctance by the government, the clause was passed by a large majority in the Commons (GRAY).

The introduction of outdoor relief represented a major change in the way the poor law operated and boards of guardians were divided in their response to it. While many welcomed the extra powers granted to them to relieve destitution in their locali-ties, others were wary of offering any outdoor relief, fearing that the demand would be more than they or the ratepayers could manage. Indeed, not giving outdoor relief 'came to be regarded as a benchmark of efficient administration and financial rectitude' (KINEALY & MacATASNEY, p. 101). This attitude reinforced the divide between poor law boards in Ulster, which managed to weather the crisis without resorting to large-scale relief outside the workhouse, and those in the rest of the country (GRANT 1990). The Poor Law Commissioners attributed what they saw as the superior quality of management in the north to the fact that guardians there were more intelligent and better educated, and that unions were smaller. More relevant was the fact that there was more accommodation within workhouses and less distress. The Belfast Board of Guardians, for example, managed to avoid resorting to outdoor relief by expanding workhouse accommodation from 1,000 to 2,643 (KINEALY & MacATASNEY).

A number of Ulster boards displayed an almost pathological aversion to outdoor relief. Rather than resort to outdoor relief when the workhouse became full in late 1847, the Lurgan Board of Guardians purchased canvas tents, while Londonderry guardians refused even to appoint relieving officers until ordered to do so by the Poor Law Commissioners (DURNIN). When elected members of the Newtownards Board persistently blocked the granting of outdoor relief, its ex-officio officers resigned, arguing that, given the rate of workhouse mortality and the degree of distress in the locality, it was unjust and uncharitable to enforce the workhouse test. The board was eventually forced to introduce outdoor relief since the Poor Law Commissioners refused to sanction an extension of the workhouse, but guardians remained deeply suspicious of potential recipients, declaring themselves determined to prevent the expectation of outdoor relief 'in that class whose great aim is to obtain the means of enjoying petty luxuries in their own filthy cabins', but who were unwilling to submit to the discipline of the workhouse (McCAVERY, p. 69). Hostility to outdoor relief, MacATASNEY (p. 74) suggests, was rooted in the fear that it would encourage idle and improvident habits and lead to a culture of dependency and ultimately to economic ruin. It was, he notes, 'as much concerned with a political ethos as with financial considerations'.

Before providing outdoor relief to the able-bodied, boards of guardians had first to obtain authorisation from the Poor Law Commissioners. The Commissioners were initially reluctant to grant such orders, believing them to be unnecessary. Instead they urged guardians to increase workhouse accommodation and to discharge the old and infirm from the workhouse, thus providing room for the able-bodied. This policy was condemned, at the time and subsequently, for discharging vulnerable people into the community without adequate resources. Having been in the workhouse for long periods, many had no homes to go to (Ó MURCHADHA 1995 & 1998; KINEALY 1994). Such cases demonstrate an uncomfortable truth: workhouses did fulfil a useful function in providing for those unable to provide for themselves. Outdoor relief was not suitable for everyone. For some, indoor relief was actually a better option.

By the end of 1847 with reports of deaths from starvation increasing, the Poor Law Commissioners were forced to issue orders extending the classes to whom outdoor relief could be provided. Within a few months, the extension of outdoor relief had been authorised in over half of the 130 unions in Ireland. Such extensions were often limited to widows with one child in the first instance, and only later extended to able-bodied men with dependent families. In 1848 orders had been granted permitting the extension of outdoor relief in 71 unions, but in only 23 of these was such relief authorised 'without distinction of class' (DONNELLY, p. 320). At the beginning of February 1848, around one quarter of the 445,456 people receiving outdoor relief were able-bodied. By April the total had risen to 638,141 and the proportion of able-bodied to one-third. The maximum number receiving outdoor relief was recorded in July 1848, when the relief lists contained over 800,000 people. By September 1848 around 2,000,000 people were estimated to have received some form of poor relief since the introduction of the new system (KINEALY 1994). Workhouse accommodation continued to increase, rising to over 300,000 places by 1851. This was due in large part to the creation of 33 new unions, bringing the total number to 163. Expanded workhouse accommodation allowed guardians to enforce the workhouse test for the able-bodied, with the result that the numbers on indoor relief reached their highest level in June 1850, peaking at 264,000 (DONNELLY).

Obsessed with the possibility of abuse, guardians and officials devoted much of their time to devising safeguards against fraud. The workhouse test was one defence, the provision of outdoor relief in the form of cooked food or wetted meal another (Ó MURCHADHA 1998). Able-bodied recipients of outdoor relief were subjected to a labour test. The Gregory clause acted as a further deterrent by discouraging small-holders from applying for any relief. Many cottiers literally starved rather than abandon their holdings. Faced with a rising number of mass evictions, ministers were forced to reassess the situation as it became clear that landed proprietors were using the Gregory clause to clear their estates. Poor law regulations were consequently relaxed in March 1848 to allow the families of land-holders, though not the land-holder, to receive relief. Landlords strongly opposed this step and did their best to ensure that boards of guardians failed to act on it (O'NEILL 1956).

As the numbers receiving relief increased so did the financial and administrative pressures on poor law boards. A number of boards proved unequal to the crisis and were dissolved by the Poor Law Commissioners and replaced by salaried vice-guardians. The original Poor Law Act had given the Commissioners the power to dissolve any board of guardians that was failing to perform its duties, but having done so they were required to order fresh elections. If the new board also failed to act effectually, the commissioners could then appoint paid officials, known as vice-guardians, to run the union. The 1847 extension act speeded up this process by providing for the immediate appointment of vice-guardians. Thirty-nine boards were dissolved during 1847-48. Indeed by the end of 1848 the chief commissioner, Edward Twistleton, was advocating the replacement of all poor law guardians by paid officials, arguing that this was the only effective means of compelling unwilling ratepayers 'to do their duty'.[3] The vice-guardians that were appointed have generally been held to have been both hard-working and efficient (O'NEILL 1956; GRAY), but since they were often obliged to adopt the same expedients as their predecessors debts continued to rise in many unions. By the autumn of 1848 the chancellor of the exchequer, Sir Charles Wood, was complaining that too many vice-guardians had been overly lavish in their distribution of outdoor relief and were encouraging idleness and dependency. A strong advocate of the principle of local responsibility, Wood argued that elected guardians would be more careful to limit outdoor relief, while their local knowledge would enable them to ensure that it went only to those who required it (HAINES). GRAY detects Wood's influence in the restoration of many of the dissolved boards in March 1849. Such influence had its limits however. A small number of boards were still in the hands of vice-guardians in 1850, suggesting that the latter were removed only when the Commissioners felt that it was safe to do so.

1848 saw a growing divide in Ireland between those areas where the Famine was largely over and the distressed unions in the west where a fourth year of food shortages had disastrous consequences. The Poor Law Commissioners had declared 22 unions in the far south and along the west coast to be 'distressed' and thus under the terms of the 1847 amendment act entitled to financial assistance, but it was clear by 1849 that many unions were simply unable to collect sufficient rates to finance the amount of relief required. The government's response was to provide a grant of £50,000 to be distributed in the distressed unions, together with the loan of a further £100,000. This was to be repaid by means of a rate of 6d in the pound to be levied on all rateable property in Ireland. In 1850 a further levy of 2d was made. By making famine relief a national but not an imperial charge, it has been argued, the rate-in-aid revealed the hollowness at the heart of the act of union (KINEALY 1994). Had the political union of 1800 been complete, the rate-in-aid would have been levied 'not on Ireland alone but on England, Scotland and Wales as well' (O'NEILL 1956, p. 248). At the same time, the acknowledgement that some unions could not be expected to support their own poor represented a departure from a fundamental principle of the poor law, that the cost of relief should be borne by the locality. Believing that the government's failure to ensure that the poor law was adequately and equitably funded had placed him in a position 'that no man of honour or humanity can endure', Twistleton resigned over the issue (GRAY, p. 314; HAINES, p. 520). The rate-in-aid bill was bitterly received in Ireland, where it was condemned as unconstitutional and unjust. Irish Tories complained that 'prudent and active landowners' in the north were being forced to support the 'improvidence and negligence of proprietors in the west and south'.[4] Opposition was strongest in Ulster where, it was claimed, ratepayers would be particularly hard hit. However a campaign to resist the collection of the rate was only partially successful and, while rate arrears were proportionately higher in Ulster than in other provinces, the imposition of the levy was never seriously disrupted.

(b) *Assisted emigration under the poor law*
Emigration had long been proposed as a solution to the problem of over-population, and state-assisted emigration had formed a key element of the Whately commission's recommendations. But while British ministers were enthusiastic about emigration in principle, they were less keen on providing money to facilitate it. Under the poor law act of 1838 boards of guardians could assist poor persons who had spent at least three months in the workhouse to emigrate, with the agreement of rate-payers. In 1843 the necessity to obtain rate-payers' sanction was removed so long as two-thirds of the board agreed. Prior to the Famine, few boards had taken advantage of these provisions. From 1844 to

1846 a total of 304 paupers from 16 unions had been assisted to emigrate (KINEALY; MORAN). The fact that eight of these unions were in Ulster reflects both the well-established emigration routes from Derry to ports in Canada and the encouragement given by the poor law inspectors for the region (PARKHILL). Increased interest in assisted emigration during the Famine owed much to the presence of so many women and children in Irish workhouses. By 1848, able-bodied women outnumbered able-bodied men by two to one in workhouses in the southern provinces and by three to one in Ulster. The proportion of children in Ulster workhouses was 52 per cent in mid-1848, and between 40 and 43 per cent in the other provinces. The great fear amongst guardians was that such women and children would come to constitute a permanent drain on the rates (KINEALY 1994; McLOUGHLIN 1995; PARKHILL; MORAN).

The Poor Law Extension Act of 1847 extended the assisted emigration provisions to all paupers including those receiving relief outside the workhouse, but the number of boards making use of the provisions remained small. It was only when external funding became available that boards of guardians took action in any significant numbers. A scheme funded by the Australian government to send orphan girls to Australia, established in 1848, proved so popular that British ministers encouraged the Australian authorities to set up a second scheme the following year. The project was brought to an end in 1850 after complaints from the colonial authorities that the girls selected for emigration were both disreputable and untrained in domestic duties. Most accounts suggest that the scheme, under which over 4,000 women travelled to Australia, benefited both the emigrants and the boards of guardians who sent them (McCAUGHLIN; PARKHILL; MORAN). However, KINEALY (1994, p. 327) brands it a failure, arguing that the needs of the colonists and the pauper emigrants 'were made subservient to the desire of the British government to promote emigration' at no cost to itself.

Ministerial efforts to initiate large-scale assisted emigration through the creation of an emigration fund of £5 million to be spent through the agency of poor law boards were blocked by the Treasury. A less ambitious scheme to boost emigration from the distressed unions by means of a rate-in-aid coupled with a government loan of £1 million failed to win cabinet approval (McDONAGH, GRAY). The only official encouragement to emigration came in the form of a further amendment to the poor law in 1849 that allowed guardians to apply to the Poor Law Commissioners to borrow money for the purpose of assisting people who had been in the workhouse for at least a year to emigrate. The result was an increase in assisted emigration from poor law unions. Over 2,500 people were assisted between August 1849 and March 1851, mostly to travel to Canada, as compared to 871 people assisted in the period from September 1848 to September 1849. Only a relatively small number of unions were involved, and these tended to be the more prosperous ones. Thus Baltinglass Board of Guardians sent out 305 paupers, Naas 305 and Athy 200 (MORAN).

There was a further increase in the numbers receiving assistance in the immediate post-Famine period, when guardians were actively seeking to empty workhouses of those inmates who threatened to become a permanent drain on union resources. In 1851-2 boards of guardians assisted over 3,000 people to emigrate, around two-thirds of whom were women. Once again a relatively small number of relatively prosperous unions was involved. Those sending out large groups included Cork, Dungannon, Newcastle, Nenagh, Carlow and Rathkeale. The schemes proved popular amongst the poor. A rumour circulating in 1851 that the Kilrush guardians had received a grant for assisted emigration led to a rush of people seeking admittance to the workhouse. Unions generally made good arrangements for the emigrants, providing them with clothes and money and, in many cases, providing a chaperone to accompany young female emigrants on their journey (MORAN).

Assisted emigration from poor law unions peaked in 1853-54. The Poor Law Commissioners had decided to make the remainder of the rate-in-aid fund available to the most hard-pressed unions in the west and south-west for this purpose, whilst large urban unions were continuing to use emigration to reduce the number of women and unaccompanied children in the workhouse. In 1854, 3,794 people were assisted to emigrate from

Irish workhouses at a cost of £22,651, of which £10,000 came from the rate-in-aid fund. Numbers declined after 1854 to between 500 and 800 per annum and remained at this level for the rest of the decade. As the economic situation in Ireland improved and the workhouse population shrank, assisted emigration became less attractive to Irish guardians, particularly as new regulations governing conditions on passenger ships to Canada were increasing the cost of fares. Adopted by boards of guardians as an economic remedy to the problems facing them, rate-assisted emigration proved more successful than landlord-assisted schemes, being better organised and involving more manageable numbers, with no more than 3,000 people sent out in any one year. For those involved, particularly the young women, emigration to North America, 'was an opportunity beyond their wildest dreams, a chance to make a new life for themselves away from the stigma of having been a pauper inmate' (MORAN, p. 158). As a response to the crisis, PARKHILL (p. 96) concludes, assisted emigration was too little too late, but 'the guardians did as well as the crippling circumstances permitted'.

(c) *Agency and entitlement*
Poor people in Ireland were adept at utilising the relief system, making calculated choices about how, when and where to apply for assistance. This remained the case throughout the Famine. Since the able-bodied became eligible for outdoor relief once the workhouse was full, people would delay seeking admittance until the house was nearing capacity in the hope of being granted outdoor relief (Ó MURCHADHA). In order to discourage such applicants the Londonderry Board of Guardians ordered that anyone admitted to the workhouse should be compulsorily detained for a minimum of two months (DURNIN). Popular reports about the state of individual workhouses influenced the actions of potential applicants. The New Ross workhouse acquired such a bad reputation that, rather than enter it, people travelled to Waterford or Dungarvan (BYRNE). Poor conditions could provoke protests amongst workhouse inmates who demanded improvements. Women appear to have been particularly active in this respect. While male inmates in the Birr workhouse contented

themselves with complaining about reduced rations in December 1848, 500 of their female cohabitants rioted, throwing bread and utensils about the hall and threatening to tear down the building (T. O'NEILL). Bad food prompted a number of disturbances by the female inmates of Athlone workhouse in 1850, as a result of which the quality of the stirabout was improved by the addition of a portion of rice or oatmeal (B. O'BRIEN). Such protests were often less successful when smaller numbers were involved. In August 1850 a number of women in Dungarvan workhouse went on strike and refused to do any more of the workhouse washing until they had been fed. They were discharged (FRAHER).

The issue of entitlement was central to the administration of relief but has received little attention from historians. It is important to distinguish here between the concept of entitlement as used by modern economic historians, and the concept as used by poor law officials and historians. In seeking to explain why famines occur, the economist Amartya SEN drew on the idea of 'entitlements' in order to give due weight to the crucial part played by the unequal distribution of resources. Ó GRÁDA (1997, pp. 147-8) has cautioned against applying this approach to explain excess mortality during the Great Famine, pointing out that Ireland experienced 'a classic case of food shortage' in 1846 and 1847. Maldistribution was not, therefore, the key factor. Famine deaths in western regions in 1848-9, he suggests, 'might well fit an entitlements approach better'. The work of local historians supports this conclusion. By 1848, 'suffering and even death' in west Cork, were caused 'more by lack of entitlement rather than lack of food' (HICKEY, p. 285). Entitlement in a poor law context has a related but narrower meaning and refers to the criteria that the poor were required to meet in order to possess a valid claim to relief. Because of the way the poor law was framed, the question of entitlement was one that poor law guardians were required to address every time a poor person applied for relief. Answering it could bring local sentiment into conflict with central regulations. Poor law boards that decided to provide relief outside the workhouse in the winter of 1846-7, for example, were acting contrary to poor law regulations which made no provision for outdoor relief under any circumstances. The guardians, however, maintained that people who were so obviously in need were entitled to assistance.

The pressure of the Famine revived debate about entitlement in general, and about the prior claim of the native poor in particular. In November 1846, the Cork Board of Guardians determined to discharge all workhouse inmates who were not residents of the union in order to accommodate the local poor 'who have the most natural and legal claim to admission'.[5] The following year, Belfast guardians resolved that, if driven to granting outdoor relief, they would restrict it to those who had been resident in the union for at least three years (KINEALY & MacATASNEY). Guardians throughout the country were extremely anxious to ensure that only those who were entitled to it should receive relief. O'NEILL (1956) recounts how people could be removed from the relief lists for looking too healthy or giving their ration to someone else. Erecting defences against 'the profligate abuse of outdoor relief by those who craved it', DONNELLY (p. 321) notes, 'became an unending official preoccupation'. But it is difficult to blame guardians for this when they were under constant pressure from the Poor Law Commissioners to be vigilant. The Ennis guardians were heavily criticised by the Commissioners in 1849 after an inspector found a number of paupers at a stone-breaking depot who appeared too well dressed to require relief. The board was instructed to apply the labour test more rigorously. Another inspector, praised for his humanity, had previously warned the guardians of the need for strict discipline within the Ennis workhouse to prevent it filling up with 'every lazy, scheming fellow in the country who would of course make no effort to procure support for himself as long as he could be fed in idleness'.[6] Guardians who were thought to be too lax in their administration could find themselves relieved of their duties. The reluctance of the Cashel Board of Guardians to cut back on outdoor relief in the spring of 1848, once auxiliary workhouse accommodation had become available, appears to be one of the reasons why the board was dissolved later that year (MARNANE). Some guardians, however, managed to get away with a fairly flexible interpretation of poor law regulations. In

December 1848, the Naas Board of Guardians ignored the official admonition against giving outdoor relief in cash and resolved to give 1s a week to all aged and infirm adults willing to leave the workhouse in order to create more space (KIELY). In the competition for scarce resources some people were fighting to survive, others were struggling to maintain their social status. The abuse and manipulation of relief distribution, FITZPATRICK (1995, p. 598) observes, 'is precisely what one might predict, in response to the Famine's devaluation of the customary entitlement of the slightly less poor'. He goes on to suggest that public officials who sought to prevent such abuse, such as the poor law inspector Captain Edmond Wynne, became the focus of local resentment and hostility. This is a plausible argument but we have as yet little convincing evidence to support it. As GRAY (p. 331n) notes, the 'very singularity' of Wynne's case, which prompted two parliamentary enquiries, in 1847 and 1850, 'suggests the need for caution in generalizing from such micro-studies'. Whatever the truth about Wynne's dismissal, it is difficult to feel much sympathy for a man who used his position to sexually exploit young women, or to accept FITZPATRICK's description of him as one of the 'forgotten victims of the Irish Famine'. Nevertheless, FITZPATRICK is right to point out that through the regulation of relief distribution in general, and through the operation of the poor law in particular, the state was acting as 'the defender of those with inferior entitlements, against the arrogation of further benefits by persons already better endowed'. As he notes, the practice of distributing outdoor relief in the form of cooked food was introduced because it was believed that men were selling the raw meal they received to feed their families, and using the money to buy alcohol (FITZPATRICK 1995, p. 618; 1997, p. 61).

Statistical evidence drawn from relief registers and annual returns suggests that during the Famine poor relief favoured able-bodied women over able-bodied men, but boys and elderly men over girls and elderly women. Thus women were over-represented amongst inmates of workhouses aged between 15 and 50, but under-represented amongst those aged under 15 and over 50. FITZPATRICK (1997) attributes this relief advantage to adult women's superior capability in the provision of 'psychic' services such as affection and consolation. An alternative explanation is that entitlement was linked to perceptions of relative vulnerability, male vulnerability, where it occurred without loss of masculinity, being perceived as more deserving than female vulnerability. This may also explain why men were less likely to riot in Irish workhouses. Entry to the workhouse was more damaging to men's self-esteem than to women's. Women felt less disempowered because they had less power to lose.

Assessments of the performance of poor law guardians and officials during the Famine have tended to be negative. A series of parliamentary enquiries into the local administration of poor relief in western poor law unions held in 1850-51 reported unfavourably on the role of poor law guardians, ratepayers and landlords. Such criticism was strongly rejected by local residents, who argued that it was the poor law system rather than its administrators that had proved inadequate (KINEALY 1994). Historians too have found much to censure. Ó MURCHADHA (1995, p. 42) cites the reluctance of the Limerick Board of Guardians to act on reports of severe overcrowding in the auxiliary workhouse at Mount Kennett in January 1848 as evidence of a 'callousness typical of those elements in society' who feared that proper provision for the poor 'would be at personal cost to them' through increases in poor rate. Yet, given the onerous nature of the task before them, it is perhaps unsurprising that some guardians proved unequal to the challenge. One Waterford guardian found himself single-handedly determining 600 applications for relief on a single day in March 1848. The Waterford Board was dissolved soon afterwards (BYRNE). In assessing the role of central government, historians have tended to draw a distinction between officials based in Ireland and England, with the former generally being seen as more sympathetic to the plight of the Irish poor than their colleagues in London (DALY 1986; KINEALY 1994). But it was the Poor Law Commissioners in Dublin, and poor law inspectors around the country, who insisted on the imposition of the workhouse test, and on the restriction of outdoor relief. Twistelton, HAINES points out, could be just as rigid and dogmatic in his approach as Trevelyan.

Case studies of individual unions or counties have identified examples of good and bad management on the part of guardians and workhouse officers. They have also highlighted some intriguing anomalies. Excess mortality was higher in County Offaly, for example, than in County Donegal, despite Offaly's apparent economic advantages of lower population density and higher land values. T. O'NEILL suggests that this discrepancy is due to the availability of alternative sources of income from seasonal migration and cottage industries in Donegal, and to the fact that the people were more used to, and thus more efficient at, soliciting aid from both official and non-governmental sources. If the latter point is true, it is interesting that people in Connemara, who were equally experienced in soliciting aid, seem to have been unable to capitalise on this to the same extent. Having analysed mortality rates within workhouses across Ireland, GUINNANE and Ó GRÁDA (2002, p. 62) conclude that local studies have tended to write 'national history in the guise of local history', presenting what were in fact general problems and short-comings as particular to a specific union. What is needed, they suggest, is a twin-track approach combining detailed case studies with comparative analysis at national level, thus allowing local experience to be understood in context. Few would deny that the poor law helped to alleviate the impact of the Famine. Cork city, O'MAHONY (p. 145) observes, 'benefited from the presence of the workhouse and without it the death toll would have been much greater'. It is equally clear, however, that the mechanism of the poor law could have been utilised to reduce the death toll still further had the saving of lives been prioritised over financial rectitude.

III

THE POOR LAW IN POST-FAMINE IRELAND

(a) *The aftermath of the Famine*
The immediate post-Famine period was one of retrenchment and reform. Most poor law boards reverted as quickly as possible to the welfare regime they had been operating prior to the onset of the Famine. Outdoor relief was either abolished altogether or reduced to a minimum. But if guardians were seeking to return to the past, the Poor Law Commissioners were looking to the future. The experience of the Famine had demonstrated both the efficacy of central regulation of medical facilities and the inadequacy of the voluntary system, thus opening the way to an expansion of poor law medical services that the Commissioners had been pushing for since before the Famine. The medical profession was, however, determined to limit the scope of the Commission's remit in medical matters, and used its considerable political influence to prevent county infirmaries and fever hospitals from being incorporated into the poor law system along with dispensaries (CASSELL; GEARY).

The 1851 medical charities act established a network of local dispensaries funded from the poor rate and administered by local committees composed of poor law guardians and resident property holders. The 163 poor law unions were divided into 723 dispensary districts with at least one dispensary in each district. These committees were responsible for the management of the dispensary and the appointment, subject to the approval of the Poor Law Commission, of a medical officer together with an apothecary and midwife, if required. From 1867, half the cost of medical officers' wages was met by central government. Members of the managing committee, together with the union relieving officers, were responsible for authorising medical treatment, the only criteria being that applicants had to be poor and unable to afford the fees charged by Irish physicians and surgeons. Since the normal fee was one guinea, the number of people who fell

38

within this category was considerable. Those authorised to receive treatment were given a ticket to be presented at the dispensary or, in the case of more serious cases, entitling the sick person to a home visit from the dispensary doctor. The ticket system was to come in for much criticism, not least from dispensary doctors who complained that it was abused by committee members who gave out tickets far too easily in order to maintain their influence within the locality. Despite the rigours of a dispensary doctor's life and the relatively poor salary, the post was highly sought after due to the excess of qualified medical practitioners in Ireland (CASSELL; GEARY).

The Medical Charities Act represented a major advance in the provision of medical services in Ireland, bringing 'a medical practitioner into every district in the country' and offering free medical treatment outside the workhouse (BURKE, p. 154). It also represented a significant development of the poor law system since it introduced another form of outdoor relief to Ireland. Moreover, since medical relief was not confined to the destitute, it was non-pauperising, a fact that probably helps to explain the very high take up, particularly in the early years of the system when nearly 16 per cent of the population was receiving treatment (CASSELL). The Poor Law Commissioners sought to present medical relief and poor relief as separate systems operating under different principles, but this was always an artificial distinction and over the following decades the availability of outdoor relief in a variety of different forms was gradually to undermine the workhouse test.

The ultimate objective of the Poor Law Commissioners, and of the chief commissioner, Alfred Power, in particular, was to create a comprehensive system of medical relief that would encompass hospitals as well as dispensaries. To this end the Commission pressed for the introduction of further reforms to bring county infirmaries and fever hospitals within the medical charities system. When the opposition of infirmary surgeons proved too great, the Commission adopted an alternative plan whereby hospital care would be provided for the sick poor in workhouse infirmaries. This was achieved in 1862 when the Poor Law (Ireland) Amendment Act provided for the admission of poor people suffering from non-contagious diseases to workhouse infirmaries. Difficult or complex cases could be transferred to the county infirmaries, with the cost being met from the poor rate. CASSELL (p. 128) regards the conception and realisation of state medicine in Ireland as a significant achievement. By the 1870s, the Poor Law Commission had succeeded in welding 'a hodge-podge of largely unorganised, unsupervised and uncoordinated medical facilities' into 'a rationally administered, nationwide system providing the Irish poor with the most comprehensive free medical care available in the British Isles'. GEARY (pp 215-6) is less impressed, believing that the development of Irish hospitals 'along twin or parallel lines' with workhouse infirmaries, operating separately from county infirmaries and accommodating far more patients, was a fundamental flaw in the system. By the twentieth century, he notes, there was considerable dissatisfaction with what the Irish Public Health Council termed the 'disjointed and unsatisfactory' organisation of the hospital system and there were growing calls for the separation of medical care from poor relief. The main obstacle to improved hospital care, however, was lack of funding and it is questionable whether a more co-ordinated hospital system separate from the poor law would have been better resourced or indeed better administered.

Other changes to the poor law system brought about by the 1862 Amendment Act included the abolition of the quarter acre clause with regard to indoor (though not outdoor) relief, and the introduction of a boarding out system for orphan and deserted children up to the age of eight years. An attempt was also made to resolve the controversy over the religious education of foundlings by providing that where a child had been baptised before entering the workhouse it should be educated in the religion of the godparents. These changes were widely welcomed but there were many who saw the act as a missed opportunity. Catholic clergy, led by Archbishop Cullen and supported by Irish Party MPs, had engaged in a concerted effort to persuade the government to alter the system so that the emphasis was on outdoor rather than indoor relief, arguing that this would be less degrading and more cost effective. They also objected to the catch-all nature of Irish workhouses, advocating stricter classification within the workhouse and the removal to specialist institutions of those requiring special care on account of either physical or moral infirmity. These arguments were rejected by the Poor Law Commissioners who remained convinced that any dilution of the workhouse test would result in an uncontrollable rise in the level and cost of relief and the consequent demoralisation of the poor, who would look to poor relief, rather than their own efforts, to maintain themselves and their families. The success of the Commissioners in preventing a more radical reform of poor relief in 1862 was, however, more apparent than real, for the amendment act represented a major landmark in the evolution of the poor law system. By opening up workhouse infirmaries to poor people who were sick but not destitute, and by providing for young children to be raised outside the workhouse, the act was taking the system further away from its residualist origins.

Pauper children were a focus of particular concern in the post-Famine period due to the large numbers of orphan and deserted children in Irish workhouses (ROBINS; McLOUGHLIN 1997). Philanthropists campaigned to remove as many children as possible from workhouses and to improve conditions for those who remained. Young inmates themselves protested against poor conditions and lack of opportunities by defying or evading workhouse discipline. Riotous behaviour by young women in the South Dublin workhouse in the early 1860s prompted a public debate on workhouse conditions and on the failure of such institutions to provide appropriate care for children and young adults (BURKE; CLARK). But whilst it was widely agreed that a workhouse upbringing was detrimental to the physical and moral health of the young, there was little agreement over alternative provision. Archbishop Cullen assiduously asserted the claim of the Catholic church to provide for the welfare of Catholic children. Protestant philanthropists, however, feared that Catholic-run institutions produced the same detrimental effects as workhouses, destroying individualism and self-reliance (LUDDY 1995; CLARK). Such divisions made it difficult for critics of the workhouse system to unite behind a common programme of reform. Some progress was made. The age limit for boarding-out children was gradually increased to 15 years and greater emphasis was placed on providing for the health, education and training of pauper children. A Local Government Board circular issued in 1876, for example, impressed on boards of guardians the importance of providing children with exercise and recreation outside the workhouse grounds on a daily basis (ROBINS). Nevertheless, the number of children in Irish workhouses continued to dismay philanthropists, who were still calling for an extension of boarding-out in the early decades of the twentieth century (LUDDY 1995).

The late 1860s and 1870s saw further expansion of the responsibilities of the Poor Law Commissioners and poor law guardians in the field of public health. Under the Sanitary Act of 1866, the Poor Law Commission was constituted as a national board of health responsible for all sanitary matters in the event of an epidemic, while sanitary committees composed either entirely of poor law guardians, or of guardians and ratepayers, were empowered to take action in matters such as the removal of refuse and other nuisances, the cleaning of streets, the construction of sewers and the supply of clean water. The powers of poor law guardians in these areas were extended by the Public Health Acts of 1874 and 1878. Poor law boards in rural areas were constituted sanitary authorities with statutory responsibilities that ranged from taking action against infectious disease to the regulation of lodging houses (CROSSMAN 1994). Rural guardians thus came to act as guardians not only of the poor, but of public health also.

Expansion of the poor law system, and thus of the remit of the Poor Law Commissioners, took place in the face of continued hostility from both the medical profession and the Catholic church. The former resented the authority of a body composed mainly of laymen, while the latter regarded the Commission as too English and too Protestant. Within central government, however, these same characteristics were believed to elevate the Commissioners above the sectional interests that appeared to dominate local authorities. In 1872 the Irish Poor Law Commission was abolished and its powers vested in the newly constituted Local Government Board for Ireland. Membership of the Board comprised the president, who was the Chief Secretary for Ireland, the vice-president, and three commissioners, one of whom was the Irish under secretary acting ex-officio. Since the Chief Secretary was frequently either absent from Ireland or occupied with other matters, the vice-president acted as the effective head of the Board. In creating one central authority to supervise all forms of local government, ministers were acting to assimilate English and Irish administrative practices but the impact in Ireland, where the Poor Law Commission already had a public health remit, was more limited than in England where responsibility for local administration had been shared between four different departments. As McDOWELL (1964, p. 188) notes, in personnel and outlook the Irish Local Government Board was 'the Poor Law Commission under a new name'. Nevertheless, the responsibilities of the Board were more extensive than those of the Poor Law Commission and its powers, which included the power to alter local government boundaries, greater (CROSSMAN 2006a).

(b) *Labourers' cottages*
Generally seen as a product of the land campaign, the result of 'a trade off between land for farmers and housing for agricultural labourers' (FAHEY, p. 121), the Labourers Acts (1883-1906) can also be understood as a 'logical progression' from public health legislation passed in the 1860s and 1870s (CULLEN, p. 35). The acts empowered boards of guardians to build and maintain improved housing for rural labourers resident in the locality. The cottages were originally reserved for male labourers whose principal earnings were derived from agriculture, but the definition of an agricultural labourer was later extended to include anyone who did any waged agricultural work, including women. From 1891 state subsidies were available to offset the cost of construction and these were gradually increased until, from 1906, the state met 36 per cent of loan repayments. This allowed rural authorities to build cottages at no cost to the rates and to let them at rents averaging between 1s and 1s 6d a week, around 10 per cent of a labourer's income in the 1910s. After a slow start, numbers of cottages erected increased significantly in the early decades of the twentieth century. Of the 43,702 cottages

completed by March 1914, over half had been built in the years since 1906 (FRASER).

It is often assumed that the acts had little effect to begin with because farmers were anxious to keep the number of cottages built, and thus the rate burden, to a minimum. Boards of guardians, McKAY argues, made no real effort to put the acts into operation until spurred into action by the presence of labour representatives on local councils following the 1898 Local Government Act, and the availability of generous state subsidies which reduced the burden on the rates. However, CROSSMAN (2006a) suggests that the slow rate of construction in the early years of the acts was as much a consequence of technical problems inherent in the legislation as of resistance on the part of boards of guardians. There were significant regional variations in the take-up of the acts, with boards of guardians in Leinster and Munster proving much more active than those in Connacht and Ulster. These variations have been explained with reference to a variety of factors, from the concentration of agricultural labourers in central and eastern districts to the strength of trade union activity (McKAY; CUNNINGHAM). Politics also played a part since boards dominated by the landed elite generally built fewer cottages than those dominated by tenant farmers. Analysis of the allocation of cottages has revealed the extent to which the selection of tenants reflected and reinforced local power hierarchies and social attitudes. Labourers thus found themselves having to conform to codes of behaviour, both moral and political, in order to qualify for a tenancy (SILVERMAN; CROSSMAN 2006a).

AALEN (p. 287) estimates that by 1921 the cottages were providing accommodation for around a quarter of a million people. The acts, he maintains, had 'achieved a social revolution comparable to that produced by the concurrent Irish Land Acts', contributing to a significant improvement in rural housing, and in the health of the rural population. The incidence of TB and scarlet fever declined as a result of better domestic conditions. It has further been suggested that the need for labourers to organise in order to agitate for better housing, and then to negotiate with boards of guardians over the terms of their tenancies, contributed to a decline in deference among the rural working class (McKAY; CULLEN). At the same time the cottages, which had a quarter of an acre, later increased to half an acre, of land attached, reduced the number of landless labourers, accelerating the blurring of class divisions at the bottom of the social scale, a development FITZPATRICK (1980) has identified as undermining labourers' collective strength. The Labourers Acts were unusual in a United Kingdom and a European context in addressing rural as opposed to urban housing. When government did turn its attention to the problem of urban housing in the early twentieth century, the solution was seen to lie not in the provision of good quality rented accommodation but in owner-occupation, this being perceived as the basis of stable family life (McMANUS).

(c) *Poor relief and Irish self government*
During the late 1870s and 1880s the context and character of poor law administration changed. Fought on the widest franchise of any governing body in Ireland, the annual poor law elections offered local politicians a regular opportunity to appeal to their communities for support and, where elected, to present themselves as popular representatives. In his study of poor law elections in the period from 1877 to 1886, FEINGOLD showed how the balance of power on the majority of Irish poor law boards shifted during these years from landlords to tenants. By categorising the holders of the three board offices (chair, vice-chair and deputy vice-chair) either as representatives of the landed elite, whom he identified as broadly conservative in politics, or as tenant farmers, whom he identified as radical, FEINGOLD was able to quantify both the decline in landlord influence over poor law boards and the concomitant increase in tenant radicalism. In 1877, landlords occupied 430, or 88 per cent of board offices. By 1886 this number had dropped to 245, or 50 per cent. FEINGOLD was primarily interested in the political consequences of this process, which he linked to the rise of the nationalist movement. However, he also made an attempt to analyse its social aspects. Having correlated variations in board radicalism with social factors such as religion, poverty and farm size, he came to

the conclusion that the rise of tenant radicalism was 'strongest and most thorough in its effects in those parts of the country where large farms predominated and where Catholicism was the religion of practically the entire population' (FEINGOLD, p. 223). Furthermore, the earliest instances of tenant radicalism occurred in those counties of Munster and Leinster where large tenant farmers had already established themselves as a rural elite and were impatient to realise their political aspirations. There was, significantly, no correlation between poverty and radicalism.

Developing FEINGOLD's work on the radicalisation of poor law politics, CROSSMAN (2003, 2006a) has examined the impact of this process on the conduct of poor law business. Where tenants dominated boards of guardians, unions affairs were characterised by a more confrontational relationship with central government and the adoption of more populist rhetoric. Whether this produced a more humane climate for the poor is questionable, however. The growing use of discretionary powers such as the granting of outdoor relief and the erection of labourers' cottages undoubtedly proved advantageous for people who could establish their eligibility, but the tendency to assess entitlement on the basis of behaviour rather than need resulted in the exclusion of socially marginal groups such as vagrants and prostitutes. Poor law boards, CROSSMAN (2006a) argues, provided Irish nationalists with a platform from which to promote the campaigns for land reform and home rule, and a means of demonstrating to the Irish people the potential benefits of self government through the provision of jobs and services. Nationalist guardians also presented themselves as more responsive to local concerns.

The Local Government Act of 1898 reinforced the trend towards populism by introducing a ratepayers' franchise, thus allowing a substantial proportion of the adult population to vote in local elections. Plural voting was abolished as were ex officio guardians. In urban areas, separate boards of guardians were retained while in rural areas district councillors also acted as poor law guardians. Anyone qualified to vote could also stand for election, although women were excluded from standing as county councillors. The act completed the transfer of local power that had been underway since the 1870s. The local elections of 1899 saw nationalists increase their total representation on poor law boards from around 50 per cent to 78 per cent, while that of unionists dropped from 50 per cent to 18 per cent. It also boosted the number of women guardians from 22 in 1898 to 85 in 1899 (CROSSMAN 1994). This increase, however, did little to erode the division of poor law administration along gender lines that had been evident from the first appearance of women on poor law boards in 1896. Women guardians were expected to concern themselves with issues such as diet, the appointment of female staff and the care of children (URQUHART).

(d) *The relief system in the post-Famine period*
During the 1850s the numbers receiving poor relief dropped back to pre-Famine levels. In 1849, 1,210,482 people had been in receipt of outdoor relief. Ten years later, this figure had dropped to 5,425. The figures for indoor relief fell from 932,284 to 153,706 during the same period (CASSELL). Comparison with Great Britain revealed that far fewer people were receiving relief and that Irish ratepayers were less heavily burdened than their English and Scottish counterparts. This was seen as a cause of concern by social reformers and Catholic clerics, but not by the Poor Law Commissioners, who welcomed the fact that Ireland was avoiding the profligate example of her neighbours. Relatively low levels of relief remained a feature of the Irish system throughout the nineteenth century, with around one per cent or less of the population receiving poor relief in Ireland compared to four per cent in Britain in the 1860s, and two per cent in the 1900s. The low level of relief, Ó GRÁDA (1994, p. 252) observes, reflected 'Irish poverty, not Irish well-being', adding that the numbers 'do not reflect well on the generosity of Irish poor law guardians and property owners'. However, a very different picture emerges if medical relief is taken into account, given that around 13 per cent of the total Irish population received medical relief in 1871-2 (CASSELL).

Comparing the populations of the South Dublin Workhouse pre- and post-Famine, BURKE found that there were more young people amongst workhouse inmates in 1861 than there had been in 1840. More than half (54 per cent) of a random sample of those admitted in 1861 were aged between 16 and 40 years of age, compared to 17 per cent in 1840. She attributes this change to the availability of outdoor relief for people whose advanced age prevented them from working, but it may also reflect the tendency of young people to migrate to the city in search of work. Having analysed the place of origin of inmates in the Rathdown workhouse in 1870, Ó CATHAOIR (p. 519) found a large number had migrated to the union from rural areas, confirming that 'the poor were drawn to towns'. Servants and labourers continued to form the largest occupational groups in workhouses in Dublin and Wicklow and, as in the pre-Famine period, married people were less likely to enter the workhouse than single people. BURKE also found a high turnover of inmates with the average length of stay dropping in comparison with 1848. Over a third of her sample left the workhouse within two weeks of admission, although some of these sought readmission within the same year. It is clear that, in Dublin at least, staying in the workhouse was a temporary measure. Over 90 per cent of inmates spent less than a year in the house compared to 88 per cent in 1848. A significant number of BURKE's sample emerged 'as a young, mobile group, the majority of whom spent just a short while in the workhouse' (BURKE, p. 190).

During the later part of the nineteenth century workhouses catered increasingly for the elderly and infirm, and the chronically ill. The proportion of able-bodied adult inmates declined from 35 per cent in 1851 to 16 per cent in 1871 whilst the percentage of aged and infirm increased from 7 to 26 per cent over the same period (CASSELL). Healthy children made up 28 per cent of the workhouse population in 1870 but just 14 per cent in 1900, while the percentage of inmates admitted to workhouse hospitals increased from 15 in 1850 to 33 in 1870 and 44 in 1900. As the population of the workhouse changed so did the regime within it. The punitive character of indoor relief became less pronounced and more attention was paid to the quality of care provided. From 1893, for example, the elderly were generally supplied with a small ration of tobacco, although smoking was allowed only at specified times. Elderly married couples were also permitted to remain together if they wished (LONERGAN). Workhouse diets became more varied with greater use being made of oatmeal, Indian meal and bread in addition to potatoes. Vegetable and meat soup became more common and, by 1887, 17 per cent of workhouses were serving either tea or cocoa on a regular basis. Ironically, the nutritional value of the diet deteriorated in comparison with the pre-Famine period when potatoes had formed the dominant item in workhouse diets. Potatoes, CRAWFORD (1993, p. 91) explains, 'provided higher biological value protein than the cereal substitutes used thereafter'.

The later decades of the nineteenth century also saw the development of a noticeably more Catholic ethos within poor law institutions. Members of female religious orders served as the most visible and potent symbol of Catholic influence within workhouses, with 84 workhouse infirmaries staffed by nuns by 1903. Prior to 1870 most boards of guardians had used workhouse inmates as nurses. These women were not paid but received extra rations. Concerns about poor standards of hygiene and of patient care led the Limerick Board of Guardians to investigate the possibility of handing the management of the workhouse infirmary over to the Sisters of Mercy. Despite strong opposition from the Poor Law Commissioners, who questioned the suitability of appointing untrained members of a religious order as workhouse staff, three Sisters were appointed as nurses in 1861. The number of boards of guardians opting to follow Limerick's example increased significantly during the 1880s and 1890s. This increase, LUDDY (1999, pp. 105-6)) argues, 'had much to do with the take-over of boards of guardians by Catholic nationalists in the decades after 1870'. Nationalist-controlled boards were attracted by the financial, as well as the religious, benefits of employing nuns. As LUDDY notes, nuns worked cheaply and often provided more staff than they were contracted to provide. In the early 1870s, for example, there were between eight and ten Sisters of Mercy nursing in the Limerick workhouse hospital, only three of whom were paid.

After dropping to its lowest level in 1856, outdoor relief became an increasingly important element of poor relief. The number of people relieved outside the workhouse rose fairly steadily from the 1860s so that by the end of the century the average daily number in receipt of outdoor relief exceeded the number of workhouse inmates. In 1862 the average daily total receiving outdoor relief was 6,263, with 55,610 people receiving indoor relief. In 1895 the average number in receipt of outdoor relief had risen to 56,619 while the recipients of indoor relief had dropped to 40,208 (CROSSMAN 2006a). The rise in numbers relieved outside the workhouse appears to have benefited women in particular. Over the last thirty years of the nineteenth century, the proportion of able-bodied women in Irish workhouses declined from around 12 per cent to around 7.5 per cent, while the proportion of able-bodied men remained roughly constant at around 5 per cent (CROSSMAN 2006b). Almost two-thirds of those receiving outdoor relief on 1 January 1892 were female, over half of whom were elderly.

The expansion of outdoor relief was particularly marked in Munster and Connacht. By 1895, only 35 per cent of those receiving relief in Munster on 1 January were inmates of workhouses compared to 60 per cent in 1878. Taking the total number of people relieved over the course of a year, however, the numbers relieved within the workhouse still exceeded the number relieved outside. Thus in 1895, indoor relief accounted for 72.5 per cent of the yearly total of recipients of relief in Ireland, a considerable majority but significantly reduced from the 92 per cent of recipients who had received indoor relief in 1862. The difference between the average daily total and the yearly total reflects the high turn-over in Irish workhouses with many people staying just a few days. This meant that while the number of inmates on any particular day might be relatively low, the yearly total could be considerable. Ulster unions, where guardians remained committed to the workhouse test, were the exception to the general trend. Looking at the numbers on relief on 1 January, the proportion on outdoor relief increased, but not as dramatically as in the rest of the country, rising from 28 per cent in 1878 to 45 per cent in 1895. Taking the yearly totals, 85 per cent of those relieved in Ulster in 1895 entered the workhouse compared to 70 per cent in Munster and 61 per cent in Connacht (CROSSMAN 2006a). That the aversion to outdoor relief evident during the Famine should have persisted for so long in Ulster can be attributed to the effects of religious and financial austerity combined with a slower rate of board radicalisation.

FEINGOLD (p. 179) linked rising expenditure on outdoor relief to the politicisation of boards of guardians, noting that the rise in the proportion of rate income expended as outdoor relief bore 'a striking resemblance' to the rise in the percentage of board offices held by tenants. However, as DALY (1997, p. 21) points out, this explanation 'ignores the extent of economic distress in western areas during the 1880s'. The fact that expenditure on outdoor relief in Connacht peaked in years of exceptional distress suggests that poverty was a more significant factor than politics. It is clear, however, that the power to grant outdoor relief was, as FEINGOLD (p. 178) maintained, 'a boon to nationalist guardians'. Granting 'a high case sum to evicted tenants and suspects' families' allowed them to 'reward the martyred families and exhibit their contempt for coercion or the landlord system, while revealing themselves as staunch supporters of the popular cause'. This practice has been investigated by CROSSMAN (2006a), who argues that it became an important element of nationalist strategy during the Plan of Campaign. But whilst the relief of evicted tenants undoubtedly added to the rise in expenditure on outdoor relief, typical payments being £1 a week compared to normal payments of 2s-3s, evicted tenants rarely formed more than a small proportion of the total number of recipients of outdoor relief in any union, most of whom were sick or disabled, or widows with children. The amount of attention focused on the relief of evicted tenants reflected the political controversy they provoked, not their relative numbers.

Central government also played a part in the expansion of outdoor relief. Having successfully resisted calls to relax poor law regulations in order to combat distress in the 1860s, ministers were forced to adopt a more flexible approach in 1879-81 in the face of a major subsistence crisis. The regulations governing outdoor relief were relaxed on four subsequent occasions before the end of the century to allow boards of guardians in the west to relieve the able-bodied outside the workhouse during periods of exceptional distress. By abandoning the workhouse test, albeit temporarily, central government was sending a powerful signal to poor law guardians not only in the west, but in the country as a whole. When serious distress once again threatened the west coast in 1894, Local Government Board Commissioner H.A. Robinson sought to dissuade the Liberal Chief Secretary, John Morley, from intervening. The practical effect of almost continuous ameliorative measures, he warned, 'would be finally to supersede the system of workhouse relief for the western peasantry'.[7] This warning was not heeded. Further official recognition of the claim of the western seaboard to special assistance came in 1891 with the creation of the Congested Districts Board, a body whose remit was to address the region's high levels of poverty and low levels of economic development (BREATHNACH).

(e) *Reform and revolution*

The early years of the twentieth century saw an intense debate over the future of the poor law system. Two official reviews were undertaken, the first of which, the Vice Regal Commission on Poor Law Reform established in 1903, focused on Ireland, while the second, the Royal Commission on the Poor Laws appointed in 1905, covered the United Kingdom as a whole. Both commissions concluded that the existing system of poor relief needed major reform and recommended the replacement of the mixed workhouse with a system of specialist institutions designed to cater for particular groups such as the sick, and the elderly. However, where the Vice Regal Commission envisaged retaining boards of guardians whilst transferring responsibility for the sick to a state medical service, the majority report of the Royal Commission on the Poor Laws advocated the establishment of county-based public assistance authorities which would be responsible for both health services and poor relief. No action was taken on either report, not least because it was clear there would be strong opposition to any measure of reform since local authorities objected to any diminution in their control over medical services, and the medical profession favoured a state medical service. Furthermore the political momentum was shifting away from poor law reform towards a more radical approach to poverty aimed at enabling the poor to support themselves with state aid (BARRINGTON).

Developments in the late nineteenth and early twentieth centuries saw the gradual abandonment of the discretionary social welfare system established under the poor law, and the adoption of reforms such as the 1897 Workmen's Compensation Act, the 1908 Old Age Pensions Act and the 1911 National Insurance Act which were based on a form of contractual relationship between the insured citizen and the state (WILEY).

In a phrase much quoted by historians, the first Dáil condemned the poor law system as 'odious, degrading and foreign', and pledged in the Democratic Programme of 1919 to replace it with a 'sympathetic native scheme for the care of the nation's aged and infirm'. Local elections in 1920 gave Sinn Féin control of 154 of the 160 poor law boards, many of which promptly passed resolutions expressing allegiance to Dáil Éireann and condemning the actions of the British government. But it was not until the summer of the following year, when the British government demanded that local councils must publicly recognise the authority of the Local Government Board in order to continue to receive state funding, that the Dáil was forced to devise a coherent plan for local administration. The main impetus behind the new arrangement was the need to reduce expenditure and rationalise administrative structures. This was to be achieved through the abolition of boards of guardians, the closure of workhouses, the amalgamation of unions and the transfer of responsibility for the poor and sick to county councils. At the same time, councils were instructed to dismiss their treasurers and lodge rate payments in special accounts. Not surprisingly, many ratepayers took advantage of the resulting confusion not to pay rates and most local authorities found themselves in severe financial difficulties.

Councils were slow to act on the proposed restructuring. Although many people supported the closure of workhouses and amalgamation of unions as a way of reducing expenditure and thus rates, they were less happy about the loss of local jobs. Only one county, Roscommon, was close to completing the process by the time the Truce brought hostilities to an end. Nevertheless, some progress was made in 1920-21. In Galway, for example, 10 workhouses were closed in 1921 along with the county hospital, the patients being transferred to the workhouse in Galway city, which was adapted to function as the county hospital. In Longford, the Granard and Ballymahon unions were abolished and their workhouses closed, while the Longford workhouse was converted into a county home. Monaghan saw the closure of three county hospitals and the conversion of the workhouse into a county home (BARRINGTON; COLEMAN; GARVIN). With the establishment of the Irish Free State, the county plan was extended across the country. The Local Government Act of 1925 legalised a county rate for poor relief and medical purposes and formally abolished boards of guardians everywhere except Dublin, replacing them with Boards of Health and Public Assistance. The majority of workhouses were converted into county homes or hospitals. The former provided institutional relief for the aged and infirm and for chronic invalids, with additional provision being made in some cases for groups such as lunatics, epileptics, unmarried mothers and children.

In devising and implementing the restructuring of county government, the interests of the poor and sick received little consideration. The disruption to poor law administration in 1920-22 had a largely negative impact on the poor. In County Offaly, for example, the Birr board of guardians suspended outdoor relief payments in January 1921 due to lack of funds (DALY 1998). The closure of hospitals and workhouses meant that many people had to travel further in order to access welfare services, and to deal with unfamiliar officials. A few people did benefit, however. In County Waterford the weekly outdoor allowance of the elderly was increased from 2s 6d to 5s in January 1922 (KINEALY 1992). Even after the return of political stability there is little evidence to suggest that the new arrangements were a significant improvement on those operating under the poor law, although this was in part a consequence of the economic depression affecting Ireland in the decades immediately following independence which would have imposed a strain on any welfare system. As KINEALY (1992, p. 593) observes, while independent Ireland 'now had its own system of poor relief, the transition made little difference to the quality of relief which paupers received nor did the number of people in receipt of poor relief drop significantly'. Both systems, old and new, were 'designed to deal almost exclusively with relief of poverty rather than with its causes'. Standards of health care and institutional care provided by local authorities in the 1920s and 1930s left much to be desired, supplying what FERRITER (p. 112) has described as 'continuity in neglect'.

(f) *The poor law in Northern Ireland*
The fact that poor law boards survived in Northern Ireland until 1948, well after their demise in both independent Ireland and Great Britain, reflects the inherently conservative nature of the Northern Ireland administration. Even in Northern Ireland, however, the impact of social welfare reforms, such as the introduction of old age pensions, meant that workhouses were increasingly occupied by the aged and infirm, the sick, the insane and children. On the last Saturday in March 1938, the Belfast workhouse contained 2,114 people, of whom 1,460 were in the infirmary. Of the 654 inmates in the main house, only 23 were able-bodied adults (FARRELL). Attempts were made to integrate the new insurance-based social welfare benefits with the poor law system. Under the Unemployed Insurance Act of 1931, for example, poor law boards operated as public assistance committees. Poor law guardians, however, remained faithful to poor law principles, seeing themselves as guardians of the public purse and public morality. Applicants were regularly removed from the outdoor relief lists in 1930s Derry, for example, for spending their relief payments on gambling, drinking or attending football matches (DURNIN). The rigid adherence of Northern Ireland guardians to traditional views of poverty and welfare was to bring them into conflict with central government.

The economic depression of the 1920s and 30s placed a considerable strain on poor law resources particularly in the major cities. Structural unemployment left growing numbers dependent on the poor law, either because they were uninsured, or because their insurance contributions had been exhausted. Since the able-bodied were not entitled to outdoor relief, unemployed workers were expected to enter the workhouse. Following protests by unemployed workers in Belfast in 1923-24, the Belfast Board of Guardians was persuaded to apply for an order under the 1898 Local Government Act authorising the provision of outdoor relief on account of the exceptional levels of distress in the city. Emergency relief was still being provided in 1927. Anxious to reduce the cost to local ratepayers, the guardians decided to cease payments to anyone who had been unemployed for over a year. As a result 235 recipients were removed from the outdoor relief lists. This decision caused considerable irritation within the Northern Ireland government. The Ministry of Home Affairs condemned it as 'contrary to the modern conception of social service', and reminded the guardians that they would be 'open to grave censure if it could be laid to their doors that, as a result of omnibus decisions, they had allowed individual deserving cases to be unprovided for'.[8] The guardians were unmoved and the government was eventually forced to empower the ministry to override the wishes of local boards and order the payment of outdoor relief in districts experiencing exceptional distress.

Unemployment was to become the cause of even greater conflict in the 1930s when discontent over entitlement to, and levels of, outdoor relief prompted protest marches and demonstrations in Belfast and Derry. In the summer of 1932, the Outdoor Relief Workers Committee called all those employed on relief works in Belfast out on strike, and organised a series of demonstrations including an invasion of the workhouse by 300 single men. Serious violence erupted on 10 October 1932, when armed police broke up a demonstration that had been banned by the authorities. The resultant rioting left one man dead and over 30 people injured. Under pressure from the government the Belfast guardians agreed to a substantial increase in rates of outdoor relief, which would be paid in cash rather than kind, as well as relief for single men and women living on their own. In Derry, by contrast, the authorities were able to contain popular militancy by banning marches and arresting the leaders of the unemployed, allowing the guardians to resist any significant concessions. Indeed, in 1933 the board adopted a policy of making all outdoor relief payments in kind. The following year the government transferred the assessment of the destitute unemployed from the guardian-run public assistance committees to newly created assistance boards, thus reducing pressure on the poor law system and easing tension between central and local government. The poor experienced little improvement in their situation, however. When responsibility for the uninsured poor was returned to poor law boards under the 1937 Poor Law Amendment act, which authorised the granting of outdoor relief to single, able-bodied unemployed, the majority of poor law boards simply ignored the act (DURNIN).

Both the retention of boards of guardians in Northern Ireland and the response to the outdoor relief protests have been interpreted as products of the divide and rule strategy adopted by the Stormont administration. DEVLIN argues that the government used the provision of social security to reward its own supporters and maintain pressure on the Catholic minority. Ministers forced the Belfast guardians to accede to the protesters demands in 1932 because the guardians' parsimony 'threatened the immediate goal of the hierarchy – the division of Protestant and Catholic working classes – and ultimately their strategy of retaining control of the state apparatus'. CLIFFORD has vigorously challenged this interpretation, pointing out that inequalities in poor relief were as much due to structural factors as to sectarianism, and insisting that the concessions won by the protesters were a victory for social action.

The poor law system was finally swept away in Northern Ireland as part of the reorganization of local government administration and health services that took place between 1946 and 1948. Northern Ireland followed Britain in establishing the Beveridge welfare state with universal benefits and free to all health services, but the welfare system introduced in Northern Ireland was more restrictive than that in Great Britain, with a more centralised administrative structure. This gave a greater role to appointed bodies and thus to professional and religious organisations (FAHEY & McLAUGHLIN). Boards of guardians met for the final time in July 1948, when they were instructed by the Ministry of Health and Local Government to preserve all papers and documents as 'a record of the valuable work done by poor law administration' (DURNIN, p. 554). This instruction helps to explain why the records of poor law unions in Northern Ireland are so much more extensive than those for unions in independent Ireland. Safeguarding the records of a disliked and discredited system came low on the Free State government's list of priorities.

CONCLUSION

The poor law had a significant impact in Ireland. Both directly and indirectly it affected people's lives, and the localities in which they resided, in ways that many other pieces of early nineteenth-century legislation did not. Over the period of its existence the system evolved in response to external events, most notably the Famine, to changing social attitudes, and to initiatives, such as the introduction of medical relief, that were generated from within. Efforts to introduce more wide-ranging reforms at the beginning of the twentieth century were hampered by political and religious divisions that prevented critics of the existing system from uniting behind a common programme of reform. The poor law never acquired popular legitimacy, but by the end of the nineteenth century it had acquired some degree of popular acceptance.

The broad outlines of Irish poor law history are well established. The main features of the relief system have also been delineated. We have some sense not only of who the recipients of relief were but of how they used the system. We know which groups of people were most likely to seek relief, and at what stages of their lives. There are, however, many aspects of the poor law that we do not understand. Ireland is largely absent from the historiography of the new English poor law and of European welfare. Yet a comparative framework is essential for any systematic analysis of welfare practices, whether within the United Kingdom or beyond. Further research is needed on the decision-making process generally and on issues of entitlement and eligibility in particular, as well as on the process by which the poor sought relief. We have only a vague awareness and even vaguer understanding of regional variations in relief practices. It would appear that poor law guardians in the north of the country were more in sympathy with the principles of less eligibility and the workhouse test than their colleagues in the south, and were slower to take advantage of their powers to grant outdoor relief and erect labourers' cottages. It remains unclear whether this was a result of the religious geography of the north, or of social and economic factors, or a combination of these. Having explored local experiences during the Famine years, local history now has a particular role to play in identifying the regional characteristics of poor relief in both the pre- and the post-Famine periods.

The poor law continued to influence welfare practices in Ireland even after the administrative structures it had created had been swept away. The poor in independent Ireland might have been spared the humiliation of the workhouse but they had no right to assistance and in demonstrating their entitlement to relief were still required to meet moral as well as financial criteria. Welfare states are presently under considerable pressure in Ireland and Britain, and questions of eligibility and access are once again under debate. Without an understanding of the poor law system and the historical development of poor relief, this debate will lack a crucial dimension.

NOTES

[1] Quoted in GEARY, p. 155.

[2] Quoted in WALSH, p. 25.

[3] Quoted in HAINES, p. 444.

[4] Quoted in GRANT 1990, p. 37.

[5] Quoted in O'MAHONY, p. 58.

[6] Quoted in Ó MURCHADHA 1998, p. 195.

[7] Quoted in CROSSMAN 2006a, pp. 136-7.

[1] Quoted in FARRELL, pp. 85.

SELECT BIBLIOGRAPHY

AALEN, Frederick H.A. 'The Rehousing of Rural Labourers in Ireland under the Labourers (Ireland) Acts, 1883-1919', *Journal of Historical Geography*, 12 (1986), pp. 287-306.

BARRINGTON, Ruth. *Health, Medicine and Politics in Ireland 1900-1970* (Dublin, 1987).

BLACK, R.D.C. *Economic Thought and the Irish Question 1817-70* (Cambridge, 1960).

BREATHNACH, Ciara. *The Congested Districts Board of Ireland, 1891-1923: Poverty and Development in the West of Ireland* (Dublin, 2005).

BRUNDAGE, Anthony. *The English Poor Laws, 1700-1930* (Basingstoke, 2002).

BURKE, Helen. *The People and the Poor Law in Nineteenth-Century Ireland* (Littlehampton, 1987).

BYRNE, Rita, 'The Workhouse in Waterford City, 1847-49', in COWMAN and BRADY eds, pp. 119-36.

CASSELL, Ronald D. *Medical Charities, Medical Politics: The Irish Dispensary System and the Poor Law 1836-1872* (Woodbridge, 1997).

CLARK, Anna. 'Wild Workhouse Girls and the Liberal Imperial State in Mid-Nineteenth-Century Ireland', *Journal of Social History*, 39 (2005), pp. 389-409.

CLIFFORD, Angela. *Poor Law in Ireland with an Account of the Belfast Outdoor Relief Dispute, 1932, and the Development of the British Welfare State and Social Welfare in the Republic* (Belfast, 1983).

COLEMAN, Marie. *County Longford and the Irish Revolution 1910-1923* (Dublin, 2003).

CONWAY, Thomas G. 'The Approach to an Irish Poor Law 1828-33', *Eire-Ireland*, 6 (1971), pp. 65-81.

COWMAN, Des and BRADY, Donald (eds). *Teacht na bPrátaí Dubha: The Famine in Waterford 1845-1850* (Dublin, 1995).

CRAWFORD, E. Margaret. 'The Irish Workhouse Diet, 1840-90', in Catherine Geissler and Derek Oddy (eds), *Food, Diet and Economic Change Past and Present* (Leicester, 1993), pp. 83-100.

————— 'Sickness and Starvation: the Agony of the Great Famine', *Ulster Local Studies* 17 (1995), pp. 34-49.

CROSSMAN, Virginia. *Local Government in Nineteenth-Century Ireland* (Belfast, 1994).

————— *Politics, Law and Order in Nineteenth-Century Ireland* (Dublin, 1996).

————— 'The New Ross Workhouse Riot of 1887: Nationalism, Class and the Irish Poor Laws', *Past and Present*, 179 (2003), pp. 135-158.

————— *Politics, Pauperism and Power in Late Nineteenth-Century Ireland* (Manchester, 2006a).

————— 'Viewing Women, Family and Sexuality through the Prism of the Irish Poor Laws', *Women's History Review*, 15 (2006b), pp. 541-50.

CULLEN, Frank. *Cleansing Rural Dublin: Public Health and Housing Initiatives in the South Dublin Poor Law Union, 1880-1920* (Dublin, 2001).

CUNNINGHAM, John. *Labour in the West of Ireland: Working Life and Struggle 1890-1914* (Belfast, 1995).

DALY, Mary E. *The Famine in Ireland* (Dundalk, 1986).

————— *The Buffer State: The Historical Roots of the Department of the Environment* (Dublin, 1997).

————— 'From King's County to Offaly: Dáil Éireann and Local Government during the Years of the Irish Revolution', in William Nolan and Timothy P. O'Neill (eds), *Offaly: History and Society* (Dublin, 1998), pp. 831-54.

DEVLIN, Paddy. *Yes We Have No Bananas: Outdoor Relief in Belfast 1920-39* (Belfast, 1981).

DICKSON, David. 'In Search of the Old Irish Poor Law', in Rosalind Mitchison and Peter Roebuck (eds), *Economy and Society in Scotland and Ireland 1500-1939* (Edinburgh, 1988), pp. 149-59.

DIGBY, Anne. 'The Rural Poor Law' in Derek Fraser (ed), *The New Poor Law in the Nineteenth Century* (London, 1976), pp. 149-70.

DONNELLY, James S. jr. 'The Administration of Relief, 1847-51', in VAUGHAN ed, pp. 316-31.

DURNIN, Patrick. 'Aspects of Poor Law Administration and the Workhouse in Derry 1838-1948', in Gerard O'Brien and William Nolan (eds), *Derry and Londonderry: History and Society* (Dublin, 1999), pp. 537-56.

EDWARDS, R. Dudley and WILLIAMS, T. Desmond, (eds). *The Great Famine: Studies in Irish History 1845-52* (Dublin, 1956).

FAHEY, Tony. 'Housing and Local Government', in Mary E. Daly (ed), *County and Town: One Hundred Years of Local Government in Ireland* (Dublin, 2001), pp. 120-29.

FAHEY, Tony and McLAUGHLIN, Eithne. 'Family and State', in Anthony F. Heath, Richard Breen and Christopher T. Whelan (eds), *Ireland North and South: Perspectives from Social Science* (Oxford, 1999), pp.117-40.

FARRELL, Michael. *The Poor Law and the Workhouse in Belfast, 1838-1948* (Belfast, 1978).

FEINGOLD, William. *The Revolt of the Tenantry: The Transformation of Local Government in Ireland 1872-1886* (Boston, Mass. 1984).

FERRITER, Diarmaid. 'Local Government, Public Health and Welfare in Twentieth-Century Ireland' in Mary E. Daly (ed), *County and Town: One Hundred Years of Local Government in Ireland* (Dublin, 2001), pp. 109-19.

FITZPATRICK, David. 'The Disappearance of the Irish Agricultural Labourer, 1841-1912', *Irish Economic and Social History*, vii (1980), pp. 66-92.

FITZPATRICK, David. 'Famine, Entitlements and Seduction: Captain Edmond Wynne in Ireland, 1846-1851', *English Historical Review*, 110 (1995), pp. 596-619.

———— 'Women and the Great Famine', in Margaret Kelleher and James H. Murphy (eds), *Gender Perspectives in 19th Century Ireland: Public and Private Spheres* (Dublin, 1997), pp. 50-69.

FRAHER, William. 'The Dungarvan Disturbances of 1846 and Sequels', in COWMAN and BRADY (eds), pp. 137-52.

FRASER, Murray. *John Bull's Other Homes: State Housing and British Policy in Ireland, 1883-1922* (Liverpool, 1996).

GARVIN, Tom. *1922: The Birth of Irish Democracy* (Dublin, 1996).

GEARY, Laurence M. *Medicine and Charity in Ireland 1718-1851* (Dublin, 2004).

GRANT, James. 'The Great Famine and the Poor Law in Ulster: The Rate-in-Aid Issue of 1849', *Irish Historical Studies*, 27 (1990), pp. 30-47.

———— 'The Great Famine in County Tyrone', in Charles Dillon and Henry A. Jefferies (eds), *Tyrone: History and Society* (Dublin, 2000), pp. 587-616.

———— 'Some Aspects of the Great Famine in County Armagh', in A.J. Hughes and William Nolan (eds), *Armagh: History and Society* (Dublin, 2001), pp. 809-850.

GRAY, Peter. *Famine, Land and Politics: British Government and Irish Society 1843-50* (Dublin, 1999).

GUINNANE, Timothy W. *The Vanishing Irish: Households, Migration, and the Rural Economy in Ireland, 1850-1914* (Princeton, 1997).

GUINNANE, Timothy W. and Ó GRÁDA, Cormac. 'The Workhouses and Irish Famine Mortality', in Tim Dyson and Cormac Ó Gráda (eds), *Famine Demography: Perspectives from Past and Present* (Oxford, 2002), pp. 44-64.

———— 'Mortality in the North Dublin Union during the Great Famine', *Economic History Review*, 55 (2002), pp. 487-506, reprinted in Cormac Ó Gráda, *Ireland's Great Famine: Interdisciplinary Perspectives* (Dublin, 2006), pp. 86-105.

HAINES, Robin. *Charles Trevelyan and the Great Irish Famine* (Dublin, 2004).

HICKEY, Patrick. *Famine in West Cork: The Mizen Peninsula, Land and People 1800-1852* (Cork, 2002).

INNES, Joanna. 'The distinctiveness of the English Poor Laws, 1750-1850', in Donald Winch and Patrick K. O'Brien (eds), *The Political Economy of British Historical Experience, 1688-1914* (Oxford, 2002), pp. 381-408.

KIDD, Alan. *State, Society and the Poor in Nineteenth-Century England* (Basingstoke, 1999)

KIELY, Karel. 'Naas Workhouse during the Famine', in *Lest We Forget: Kildare and the Great Famine* (Naas, n.d.), pp. 22-46.

KINEALY, Christine. 'The Poor Law during the Great Famine: An Administration in Crisis', in E. Margaret Crawford, (ed), *Famine: The Irish Experience 900-1900: Subsistence Crises and Famines in Ireland* (Edinburgh, 1989), pp. 157-75.

——————— 'The Workhouse System in County Waterford, 1838-1923', in William Nolan and Thomas P. Power (eds), *Waterford: History and Society* (Dublin, 1992), pp. 579-96.

——————— *This Great Calamity: The Irish Famine 1845-52* (Dublin: Gill and Macmillan, 1994)

——————— and MacATASNEY, Gerard. *The Hidden Famine: Hunger, Poverty and Sectarianism in Belfast* (London, 2000).

KING, Steven. *Poverty and Welfare in England 1700-1850: A Regional Perspective* (Manchester, 2000).

——————— and TOMPKINS, Alannah (eds). *The Poor in England 1700-1850: An Economy of Makeshifts* (Manchester, 2003).

LANIGAN, Anne. 'Tipperary Workhouse Children and the Famine', *Tipperary Historical Journal*, (1995), pp. 54-80.

LUDDY, Maria. *Women and Philanthropy in the Nineteenth-Century Ireland* (Cambridge, 1995).

LUDDY, Maria.'"Angels of Mercy": Nuns as Workhouse Nurses, 1861-1898', in Elizabeth Malcolm and Greta Jones (eds), *Medicine, Disease and the State in Ireland, 1650-1940* (Cork, 1999), pp. 102-17.

LONERGAN, Eamonn. *A Workhouse Story: A History of St Patrick's Hospital Cashel 1842-1992* (Clonmel, 1992).

McATASNEY, Gerard. 'The Famine in Lurgan and Portadown', *Ulster Local Studies*, 17 (1995), pp. 75-87.

———— *'This Dreadful Visitation': The Famine in Lurgan/Portadown* (Belfast, 1997).

———— 'Provision for the Poor in the Pre-Famine Era', in A.J. Hughes, and William Nolan (eds), *Armagh: History and Society* (Dublin, 2001), pp. 779-808.

McCAFFREY, Lawrence J. *Daniel O'Connell and the Repeal Year* (Kentucky, 1966).

McCAUGHLIN, Trevor. *Barefoot and Pregnant? Irish Famine Orphans in Australia* (Melbourne, 1991).

McCAVERY, Trevor. 'The Wealthy Found Wanting: Controversies over Poor Relief in the Newtownards Poor Law Union', *Ulster Local Studies*, 17 (1995), pp. 50-74.

McDONAGH, Oliver. 'The Economy and Society, 1830-45', in VAUGHAN (ed), pp. 218-41.

McDOWELL, R.B. 'Ireland on the Eve of the Famine', in EDWARDS and WILLIAMS (eds), pp. 3-86.

———— *The Irish Administration 1801-1914* (London, 1964).

———— 'Administration and the Public Services 1800-70', in VAUGHAN (ed), pp. 538-61.

MACINTYRE, Angus. *The Liberator: Daniel O'Connell and the Irish Party 1830-1847* (London, 1965).

McKAY, Enda. 'The Housing of the Rural Labourer, 1881-1916', *Saothar*, 17 (1992), pp. 27-39.

McLOUGHLIN, Dympna. 'Workhouses and Irish Female Paupers 1840-70', in Maria Luddy and Cliona Murphy (eds), *Women Surviving: Studies in Irish Women's History in the Nineteenth and Twentieth Centuries* (Dublin, 1990), pp. 117-47.

———— 'Superfluous and Unwanted Deadweight: The Emigration of Nineteenth-Century Irish Pauper Women', in Patrick O'Sullivan (ed), *The Irish World Wide*, Vol. 4: *Irish Women and Irish Migration* (London, 1995), pp. 66-88.

———— 'Pauper Children in Ireland 1840-70', in Breandán Ó Conaire (ed), *The Famine Lectures – Léachtaí an Ghorta* (Boyle, 1997), pp. 280-307.

———— 'Workhouses', in Angela Bourke et al (eds), *The Field Day Anthology of Irish Writing*, Vol. V: *Irish Women's Writing and Traditions* (Cork, 2002), pp 722-35.

McMANUS, Ruth. 'Blue Collars, "Red Forts", and Green Fields: Working-Class Housing in Ireland in the Twentieth Century', *International Labor and Working-Class History*, 64 (2003), pp. 38-54.

MARNANE, Denis G. 'The Famine in South Tipperary – Part Two', *Tipperary Historical Journal*, 1997, pp. 131-50.

MITCHISON, Rosalind. 'Permissive Poor Laws: The Irish and Scottish Systems Considered Together', in S.J. Connolly, R.A. Houston and R.J. Morris (eds), *Conflict, Identity and Economic Development: Ireland and Scotland, 1600-1939* (Preston, 1995), pp. 161-71.

MORAN, Gerard. *Sending Out Ireland's Poor: Assisted emigration to North America in the Nineteenth Century* (Dublin, 2004).

MOKYR, Joel. *Why Ireland Starved: A Quantitative and Analytical History of the Irish Economy, 1800-1850* (London, 1983).

MOKYR, Joel and Ó GRÁDA, Cormac. 'Poor and Getting Poorer? Living Standards in Ireland before the Famine', *Economic History Review*, 41 (1988), pp. 209-35, reprinted in Cormac Ó Gráda, *Ireland's Great Famine: Interdisciplinary Perspectives* (Dublin, 2006), pp. 24-47.

NICHOLLS, George. *A History of the Irish Poor Law* [1856] (New York, 1967).

NOLAN, Tom. 'The Lismore Poor Law Union and the Famine', in COWMAN and BRADY (eds), pp. 101-118.

O'BRIEN, Brendan. *Athlone Workhouse and the Famine* (Athlone, 1995).

O'BRIEN, George. *The Economic History of Ireland from the Union to the Famine* (London, 1921).

O'BRIEN, Gerard. 'The Establishment of Poor-Law Unions in Ireland, 1838-43', *Irish Historical Studies*, 23 (1982), pp. 97-120.

———— 'The New Poor Law in Pre-Famine Ireland: A Case History', *Irish Economic and Social History*, 12 (1985), pp. 33-49.

———— 'Workhouse Management in Pre-Famine Ireland', *Proceedings of the Royal Irish Academy*, C, 86 (1986), pp. 113-34.

———— 'A Question of Attitude: Responses to the New Poor Law in Ireland and Scotland', in Rosalind Mitchison and Peter Roebuck (eds), *Economy and Society in Scotland and Ireland 1500-1939* (Edinburgh, 1988), pp. 160-70.

———— 'State Intervention and the Medical Relief of the Irish Poor, 1787-1850', in Elizabeth Malcolm and Greta Jones (eds), *Medicine, Disease and the State in Ireland, 1650-1940* (Cork, 1999), pp. 195-207.

Ó CATHAOIR, Eva. 'The Poor Law in County Wicklow', in Ken Hannigan and William Nolan (eds), *Wicklow: History and Society* (Dublin, 1994), pp. 503-80.

Ó CIOSÁIN, Niall. 'Boccoughs and God's Poor: Deserving and Undeserving Poor in Irish Popular Culture', in Tadhg Foley and Sean Ryder Sean (eds), *Ideology and Ireland in the Nineteenth Century* (Dublin, 1998), pp. 93-99.

O'CONNOR, John. *The Workhouses of Ireland: The Fate of Ireland's Poor* (Dublin, 1995).

Ó GRÁDA, Cormac. 'The Heights of Clonmel prisoners 1845-9: Some Dietary Implications', *Irish Economic and Social History*, 18 (1991), pp. 24-33.

Ó GRÁDA, Cormac. *Ireland: A New Economic History 1780-1939* (Oxford, 1994).

———— 'The Great Famine and Other Famines', in Cormac Ó Gráda (ed), *Famine 150: Commemorative Lecture Series* (Dublin, 1997), pp. 129-58, reprinted in Cormac Ó Gráda, *Ireland's Great Famine: Interdisciplinary Perspectives* (Dublin, 2006), pp. 196-216.

O'MAHONY, Michelle. *Famine in Cork City: Famine Life in the Cork Union Workhouse* (Cork, 2005).

Ó MURCHADHA, Ciarán, 'Limerick Union Workhouse during the Great Famine', *The Old Limerick Journal*, 32 (1995), pp. 39-43.

———— *Sable Wings over the Land: Ennis, County Clare, and its Wider Community during the Great Famine* (Ennis, 1998).

O'NEILL, Thomas P. 'The Organisation and Administration of Relief, 1845-52', in EDWARDS and WILLIAMS (eds), pp. 209-59.

O'NEILL, Timothy P. 'The Famine in Offaly', in William Nolan and Timothy P. O'Neill (eds), *Offaly: History and Society* (Dublin, 1998), pp. 681-732.

Ó TUATHAIGH, Gearóid. *Ireland before the Famine 1798-1848* (Dublin, 1972).

OXLEY, Deborah. 'Living Standards of Women in Prefamine Ireland', *Social Science History*, 28 (2004), pp. 271-95.

PARKHILL, Trevor. '"Permanent Deadweight": Emigration from Ulster Workhouses during the Famine', in E. Margaret Crawford (ed), *The Hungry Stream: Essays on Emigration and Famine* (Belfast, 1997), pp. 87-100.

ROBINS, Joseph, *The Lost Children: A Study of Charity Children in Ireland 1700-1900* (Dublin, 1980).

SEN, Amartya K. *Poverty and Famines* (Oxford, 1981).

SILVERMAN, Marilyn. *An Irish Working Class: Explorations in Political Economy and Hegemony, 1800-1950* (Toronto, 2001).

STRAIN, R.W.M. *Belfast and its Charitable Society: A Story of Urban Social Development* (Oxford, 1961).

URQUHART, Diane. *Women in Ulster Politics 1890-1940* (Dublin, 2000).

VAUGHAN, W.E. (ed). *A New History of Ireland.* Vol. V: *Ireland under the Union, I, 1801-70* (Oxford, 1989).

WALSH, John, 'The Great Famine in the Callan Union', in *The Famine in the Kilkenny / Tipperary Region: A History of the Callan Workhouse and Poor Law Union, 1845-1852* (Kilkenny, 1998).

WILEY, Miriam M. 'Health, Housing and Social Welfare', in Kieran A. Kennedy (ed), *From Famine to Feast: Economic and Social Change in Ireland 1847-1997* (Dublin, 1998), pp. 50-61.

WOODS, Audrey. *Dublin Outsiders: A History of the Mendicity Institution 1818-1998* (Dublin, 1998).

MIC LIBRARY
WITHDRAWN FROM STOCK